ATTRACTING LASTING LOVE

Breaking Free of the 7 Barriers that Keep You Single

By

ROY BIANCALANA

This book is published by Roy A. Biancalana

Printed in Tampa, Florida

Cover designed by Diane Vivian
http://www.mycreativeartistry.com

First Printing: November 2014

ISBN: 978-0-578-15231-8

Visit Roy Biancalana's website:

www.coachingwithroy.com

Besides this and his first book, Roy has many high-quality, video-based eCourses designed to support the creation and development of conscious, loving relationships. These courses are 5-7 hours long and include everything Roy knows on their subjects. Here is just a sample of what's available now on Roy's website:

VIDEO-BASED ECOURSES:

Attracting Lasting Love
A Conscious Approach to Finding Your Life Partner

Finding Love Online
From Horror Stories to Love Stories—in 60 Days

The Silver Lining Blueprint
A Conscious Approach to Finding Love After 50

The Radiant Woman
Being the Woman that Evokes a Man's Full Devotion

The Superior Man
Being the Man Every Woman Wants and the World Desperately Needs

Dating in the Digital Age
Finding Your Soulmate without Losing Your Soul

READ ROY'S FIRST BOOK

Relationship Addiction—A Memoir
How One Man "Sobered Up" from One of the World's Most Common Addictions and How You Can Too

<u>DEDICATION</u>

To my lovely wife, MaryMargaret:

Words cannot describe the depth of my appreciation for your loving
support and your unwillingness to let me skate.
You are a joy and a pain in the ass,
and I wouldn't have it any other way.

I love you.

TABLE OF CONTENTS

BARRIER FOUR—COMPLETION
Making Space for Love to Appear
73

BARRIER FIVE—(de)CONSTRUCTION
Recognizing and Releasing Your Relationship Persona
95

BARRIER SIX—COMPETENCY
Awakening Your Masculine or Feminine Essence
125

BARRIER SEVEN—CREATION
The Art of Effortless Manifestation
203

CONCLUSION
Let Go
227

ACKNOWLEDGEMENTS
228

APPENDIX I
The Dating Manifesto
229

ABOUT THE AUTHOR
231

A NOTE FROM THE AUTHOR

Dear Reader,

I can only imagine how you're feeling as you begin this book. I'm guessing that this isn't the first resource you've turned to for wisdom on how to attract lasting love, and since you're reading this, they obviously haven't worked.

So you're probably frustrated, discouraged and maybe even skeptical that this book won't help either. I understand, but I want to encourage you not to lose hope. I'm going to introduce you to a very different approach to finding your life partner, one that not only worked in my life, but also in the lives of my clients.

The Prologue tells the story of how I met my wife and how I eventually proposed to her. The rest of the book describes what we did in our personal lives—*before we ever met each other*—that made those moments possible.

So the premise of this book is simple: If you do what we did, if you fully commit to the approach outlined in the pages that follow, you too will attract lasting love, because—and I mean this sincerely—*it's not about us.*

We're nothing special. It's not our karma to find love, the stars weren't aligned for us and we didn't get lucky. *It's about the approach we took, and if you do the things we did, you can have the same results we got.*

Roy Biancalana
Orlando, Florida
November 2014

PROLOGUE

Popping The Question

The Whitehall Hotel, Chicago, Illinois
October 26, 2007

I led MaryMargaret to believe that the romantic weekend we were spending together at a swanky hotel in downtown Chicago was to celebrate her birthday and our one-year dating anniversary.

It was much more than that.

I should tell you a little bit about MaryMargaret and how we met before I go on with the story.

Quite simply, she's the most delicious woman I've ever met. Like a vat of hot fudge that you want to dip your hands into and smear all over your face, she's warm, sweet, and gooey.

We met one year before at a spiritual growth conference just outside of Chicago. She was there because of the subject matter—conscious relationships—but also to fulfill her continuing education requirements as a licensed clinical social worker and therapist. I was there because the keynote speaker was Dr. Kathlyn Hendricks, the wife of my friend and mentor, Dr. Gay Hendricks. Even though I knew Gay well, I had never met Kathlyn, so when I heard she was in town teaching, I went to meet her, and of course, to learn from her.

I arrived early and had a nice chat with Kathlyn on the speaker's stage, and when the event was about to begin, I said my goodbyes, turned and scanned the audience, looking to sit next to the most beautiful woman in the room. (Hey, I was there to learn, but what the hell!) As I scanned the crowd, she caught my eye. The image of her sitting there remains imprinted in my mind to this day. Off to my left, about 10 rows back and 3 seats in, was this beautiful brunette, sitting peacefully with her legs crossed and holding a Starbucks cup of something.

And the seat next to her was open.

Well, I'm surprised Kathlyn didn't confront us from the stage because, while we were listening to her (sort of), we were flirting and laughing with one another throughout her entire presentation. For example, I remember when MaryMargaret first told me her name, she quickly followed that with, "but I'm not a nun."

(You had me at hello.)

We were having a great time until Kathlyn's presentation became experiential, meaning, she wanted us to pair up with someone so that we could practice the conscious relationship principles she was teaching, instead of just learning about them.

Crap.

Doing body-centered practices with a complete stranger is awkward enough, but when your practice partner is someone you're extremely attracted to, and overtly flirting with, it becomes downright terrifying.

The first practice Kathlyn had us do together was something called *Creative Joint Play*. I cannot tell you how much I hate this practice. Kathlyn said its purpose was to physically and energetically unkink the body so that the creative juices can flow, preparing the way for learning and change. I say its purpose is to embarrass the hell out of a 47 year-old man in front of a beautiful woman, but I'll let you be the judge.

The way *Creative Joint Play* works is that you start with one joint in the body, usually the jaw, and move that joint in every conceivable direction. Then you add in another joint, then another joint, and then another joint, until every joint in the body is moving as wildly and freely as possible—contorting, twisting, bending, jerking—at the same time!! Can you picture that? You look like an absolute freak! Remember how Elaine danced on *Seinfeld*? Well, multiply that by ten and you get the picture. And we're doing this—*together!* (Don't ever complain to me about embarrassing moments on your first date. I win.)

And it gets worse.

Having been humiliated...um, I mean...unkinked and ready for change, Kathlyn, then, introduced two more conscious relationship practices: *Persona Play* and *Tossing*. A *persona* is a "mask," a false self, a façade we wear in relationships. It is not the real you, but the "person" you believe you have to be in order to attract or sustain an intimate relationship.

The truth is that almost all of us relate as our persona self rather than as our authentic self. (Obviously, this is a major barrier to attracting lasting love, and we'll talk about it later in the book.) Our personas must be dropped and part of the way we do that is through something called, *Persona Play*.

Kathlyn had us pair up—again!—and take turns sharing the names of our personas with one another and explaining how they operate in our lives.

14

And to make it "fun," each couple was given a balloon, and after you finished your turn describing your persona, you "tossed" the balloon to your partner (we batted it like a volleyball), signifying that it was their turn to talk about their persona.

Looking back on it now, it's pretty funny. One minute I'm flirting with this beautiful, sweet, gooey woman, trying to impress her with my spirituality and sense of humor, and the next minute we're sharing a full-blown *conniption fit* together, followed by a practice that revealed our false, phony, fear-driven ways of operating in the world! Exactly how most first dates go, don't you think?

However, we had fun with it or at least it seemed that way on the surface. We were laughing and listening and asking follow up questions, generally enjoying the "volley-balloon" practice with each other, but inwardly, I felt exposed. Yet at the same time, it was strangely freeing to be so real and I began feeling connected to her. Weeks later, I learned she felt the same way.

That's how we met. No cheesy pick up lines, no strategies, no profiles, no games. We met serendipitously, in the flow of life, and as we did, we each took the risk of being real right from the very beginning.

(Note: Neither one of us knew that the other had previously been doing significant inner growth work that made us willing to be so open with each other. There was a lot of "junk" that had been cleared out of our lives before this moment. That "clearing" is what this book is all about.)

Fast forward one year, and we're here in the luxurious Whitehall Hotel, getting ready for what she thinks is simply a romantic evening together.

"Before we go, there's something I want to ask you," I said. She sat down, sensing something, but definitely not knowing what was about to happen, partly because I've concealed my plan brilliantly, but mostly because I grabbed a balloon out of my overnight bag and began to blow it up. That sort of threw her off.

This was the very same balloon we had played with a year ago. I had saved it. As I blew it up, I was careful to position the balloon in such a way that she couldn't see the four words I had written on it. I tied it off and said, "Do you remember that crazy *Persona Play/Tossing* game we did together one year ago?" She nodded, still sort of confused.

"This is the same balloon. I saved it." She smiled, putting her hand on her heart, obviously touched.

"Can we play again, just for a minute?" Not waiting for a response, I approached her and got down on one knee. The plan was to bat her the balloon, she'd read those special 4 words and say "YES!," and we'd have wild sex before dinner. I thought it was an awesome plan, but when I batted the balloon...wait for it...the damn thing popped!

I was crushed. Devastated is more accurate.

I picked the tattered thing up off the floor, moaning in disappointment, and handed it to her, somehow trying to salvage the moment.

In a broken-hearted voice, I said, "Ahhhh, can you read what it says?" She couldn't. It was too torn up.

I took the ring out of my pocket and said, in sort of an exasperated voice, "MaryMargaret, will you marry me?"

Then it dawned on me...I had *literally* popped the question.

INTRODUCTION

Rumi's Way

"Your task is not to seek love, but merely to seek and find all the barriers within yourself that you have built against it."

~ Rumi
13th Century Mystic Poet

George Bailey had a plan for his life. He had big dreams. He was going to get out of the little town of Bedford Falls and see the world. Italy, Greece, the Parthenon, the Coliseum, and then after college, he would build skyscrapers, airfields and bridges a mile long. It was, indeed, going to be a wonderful life.

It didn't work out the way, though. Not even close.

When his father died, George got wind of Potter's evil schemes, so he put his travel and college plans temporarily on hold and took over the family business. He would run things until his brother finished college, then he'd resume his plans of seeing and changing the world. But that didn't work out either.

Even his honeymoon plans were thwarted when there was a run on the bank. He had to use his personal savings to keep the business afloat and the town from falling into the hands of Potter. Nothing was going according to plan.

George Bailey finally hit rock bottom when his senile Uncle Billy lost track of the bank's money, and not only was George facing bankruptcy, he was likely headed to prison. Talk about a life that didn't go according to plan.

Broken, despairing and hopeless, about to give up on life, all he could do is pray, "Show me the way."[1] That's when, Clarence, his wingless guardian angel, showed up, and well, you know the rest of the story.

---

[1] The electronic version of this book allows the insertion of links to enhance the learning and make it fun, and it happens frequently throughout the book. Here's the scene where George prays for guidance: http://bit.ly/1lqxFKm

Without being overly dramatic, I wonder if you can relate to George. I'll bet your love life has not gone according to plan. Tell me, did you ever imagine you'd be reading a book like this—*at this point in your life*? Of course not. You were either supposed to meet someone in college or soon after, fall in love and live happily ever after—or—you were going to get your career established first, and then in your early 30's or so, you'd meet someone, settle down and maybe even start a family.

I don't know what your plan was, but I'm pretty sure it wasn't any of the following:

- Divorced, possibly a single parent, forced to start over
- Professionally successful, but disappointed by a string of failed relationships
- Betrayed and broken-hearted, wondering if you can open your heart again
- In your late 30's or early 40's, no partner in sight, with your biological clock ticking
- Single, quite able to attract partners, but never the right ones
- At mid-life and alone, terrified of online dating, hating bars and clubs, yet not knowing any other option
- Never been married and feeling that it's hopeless, secretly wondering if something's wrong with you
- Divorced or widowed, terrified of going "out there" and facing the modern dating scene

So, I imagine you can relate to George Bailey, at least in terms of how your love life has panned out. It's hasn't been a wonderful life. You're single (for whatever reason) and you don't want to be, and although you're not about to jump off a bridge, you probably feel that your plans of meeting a wonderful man or woman and creating a healthy, passionate, lasting relationship with them is hopeless, or least a long shot. Why? Because you've tried *everything*! and none of it's worked—and now you're reading this damn book!

Listen, I get it. I really do. I got married when I was 24. My wife and I were supposed to have this exciting, highly sexual relationship, gallivanting around the country playing on the PGA Tour making truckloads of money. It didn't turn out that way. Yes, I did get on the Tour, but I flamed out and quit after 2 years, not having enough money to fill a toy Tonka Truck. And as for that exciting, highly sexual marriage I envisioned? That didn't happen either. It fizzled into a functional, platonic thing. To say I was discouraged would be an understatement. Despairing is more like it.

So what did I do? I came up with a new plan, of course, which was to have an affair.[2] Well, that blew up in my face in spectacular fashion and I went through a divorce. But since I thought I loved my mistress, we worked things out, and 18 months later, we became engaged. Now the plan was to have that exciting, sexual relationship with her. However, since that relationship was built on fear and insecurity, it fell apart and she dumped me 6 months before the wedding.

I was a basket case. I came unglued. I was an absolute mess. And that called for a new plan.

I decided to get online and date as many women as possible, thinking that would help me get over my fiancée and the incredible emptiness and loneliness I felt. (Don't laugh. It's not polite.) To make a long story short, I ended up creating my own rock bottom moment, similar to George's, only instead of taking my own life by jumping off a bridge, I had my girlfriend thinking of doing it for me with a 7-iron, while we vacationed at an au naturel resort in the Caribbean. [3]

So, there I was, a 46 year-old man, divorced from his wife, dumped by his fiancée, nearly dead at the hands of his girlfriend, and riddled with drama from dating, online and otherwise.

This was not the plan. This was not the way my life was supposed to turn out.

A Gift From God

I had tried every approach known to man on how to attract lasting love. Okay, yes, some of those approaches were twisted—I admit that—but most of the ways I tried to find my ideal partner were more of the socially acceptable and conventional kind.

The point is, none of it worked for me. I was at the end of my rope, out of answers and seriously wondering if I'd ever be in a fulfilling, lasting relationship. I was depressed, hopeless and filled with despair. I'm not exaggerating. But that was a good thing. *In fact, it was the best thing that's ever happened to me.* Rock bottom was a gift from God, for the pain and despair I felt caused me to do two life-changing things.

---

[2] I tell the complete story in my first book, *Relationship Addiction—A Memoir: How One Man "Sobered Up" from One of the World's Most Common Addictions and How You Can Too.*

[3] For this story, see the Prologue in the book mentioned in footnote #2.

First, I reached out for help. Like George Bailey praying, "show me the way," I said a prayer of sorts too. George's answer came in the form of *Clarence*, his guardian angel; my answer came in the form of *Diana Chapman*, my guardian angel (coach).

The second thing that the pain and despair caused me to do was open my heart to a very different approach to attracting lasting love. Quite honestly, I would NEVER have been open to what I've come to call, *the conscious approach to finding your life partner*, if I hadn't already come to the conclusion that all the conventional approaches didn't work. The conscious approach is only available to those who are completely out of options. You only become interested in, or in fact, eligible for, the conscious approach when you've hit relationship rock bottom.

If you have even the slightest interest in any of the 6 conventional approaches to finding love outlined below, then the conscious approach will not work for you. Now, I'm pretty sure you're already at that point or you wouldn't have picked up this book. But we have to make sure, because:

The Conscious Approach will only work if it's your only approach.

You must be completely done with all the common and conventional approaches to finding love—before the conscious approach can work. As Jesus said, "no one puts new wine into old wineskins."[4] So before I introduce the conscious approach, I want to explore the conventional approaches with you and see if you're willing to abandon them completely and fully commit to the conscious approach.

6 F-Words
The conventional approaches to finding a life partner can be described by 6 F-Words.

1. Fate: *The Defeated Approach*
This first conventional approach, Fate, is a fairy-tale, romantic comedy-type hope that somehow, somewhere and in some mysterious way, the stars will align perfectly and fate will bring two people together. It's rooted in The Soulmate Syndrome, the belief that there's one special person destined for us and fate will one day allow us to find one another.

---

[4] Mark 2 :22

I sometimes call it the *Reese's Peanut Butter Approach*. Remember that old commercial?[5] Someone's walking with chocolate and they bump into someone walking with peanut butter? The two get mixed and they discover they're delicious together! It's Fate! Great commercial; lousy approach to finding love.

People who are consciously or unconsciously using this approach say things like, "Well, I just haven't crossed paths with the right person yet," or "It's not God's will for me to find someone yet," or "Someday it's going to happen. I just have to be patient."

Now, there is a tiny-weeny, itsy-bitsy grain of truth in there. We are not in total control of the universe. But very rarely does a person who's deeply grounded in the Eternal Now say things like that. This sweet-sounding, pseudo-spiritual, I'm-relying-on-fate approach masks a defeatist attitude. It's a cop-out. Inwardly they've given up and they're playing the victim, blaming their relationship status on events that are beyond their control.

2. Fishing: *The Desperate Approach*

This second conventional approach, Fishing, is a saturation strategy. It says if I put my "hooks" into enough "ponds," I'm liable to catch something. (And that's true. But in my experience, what you catch you'll want to throw back!)

People who use this approach join multiple online dating sites, they frequent pick up bars, join Meet Up groups and attend lots of single's events. This approach is sort of the polar opposite of the Fate approach. With Fate, you sit back and do nothing, waiting on the gods. With the Fishing approach, you leave no stone unturned which is why I call this the desperate approach.

I was not a Fate guy. It does not fit my personality, but the Fishing approach sure did. I was on *Match, E-Harmony, Yahoo Personals* and *Great Expectations*—at the same time. Hell, I would have joined *J-Date* and even *OurTime*, if I had been eligible. In my mind, it was a numbers game.

3. Fixed Up: *The Delegating Approach*

If Fate and Fishing don't work, then we sometimes turn to others for help.

There are those who've met their mates by being fixed up. However, the vast majority of people who actively use the Fixed Up approach are

---

[5] Enjoy. http://bit.ly/1pADOXe

coming from a disempowered, victim state of consciousness. It often sounds like, "I don't know how, or where, or what it even takes to meet someone. I've gone through everyone at work and in my social circle. I just don't know what to do. Can *you* help me?" Translation: can you do it for me? There is a disowning of responsibility hidden in this approach which is why I call it the delegating approach.

In other words, with the Fixed Up approach, as is true with all the conventional approaches, the answer to finding a partner is outside of us, while the conscious approach asks us to turn inward and seek to understand how our beliefs, energies, personas and unconscious commitments are keeping us single.

4. Fake It: *The Deceptive Approach*

Hands down, and there's not even a close second, the Fake It approach was my go-to approach. I would become a chameleon, morphing into whoever or whatever I needed to be in order to get the attention and affection of a beautiful woman. Most of us are pretty good at this; I was an absolute genius at it.

Are you liberal or conservative? Me too. Are you a Christian? I'll quote scripture. Are you a new ager? Namaste. Are you afraid of angry men? I'm Eckhart Tolle. Do you want an alpha male? I'm Clint Eastwood. Do you want to take it slow? That's amazing. So do I!

Do you need a Mr. Mom type? I love kids, especially yours. Do you need someone to listen? I'll be your therapist. Are your shoulders tight? I'll be your Masseuse. Do you need a surrogate father? I change diapers. Are you too busy to clean your house? That's amazing because I love vacuuming!

Faking it is one of the most common approaches to attracting a partner. We become someone we're not, which is why it's called the deceptive approach. However, we're usually not consciously aware that we're doing this. I know I wasn't. I just thought that's how you get someone to love you.

5. Former Lovers: *The "Done That" Approach*

Another conventional approach to finding a partner is to go back to former lovers and try again. We recycle, which is why I call it the "been there, done that" approach.

I've found that the Former Lovers approach is a result of RAS— Relationship Alzheimer's Syndrome. When we're not in a relationship, and we begin to feel those empty, lonely sensations, we tend to forget, overlook or sugarcoat the reasons why it didn't work out with someone in the past. When that happens, the attraction reignites, and before you know it, you're having sex and thinking you're in love again. In time, however, the reasons that originally drove the two of you apart resurface and you realize you've made a huge mistake. Recycling rarely works. Watch out for RAS.

6. Formulas: *The Dependent Approach*

The world is filled with tips, techniques, tricks and tactics. And I understand that. Relationships are hard so we seek easy answers, simple strategies, quick fixes and cookie-cutter formulas. But in doing so, we move away from our hearts, our authenticity, our true emotions and our inner knowing. Instead, we become dependent on something or someone outside of ourselves.

The conscious approach that I'm about to describe is not a how-to formula. It's a call to awaken; it's a journey of self-discovery. Are you ready for the conscious approach? Are you done with the 6 F-Words? Are you sick and tired of the game?

Rumi's Way

What I have learned from my own personal experience and in my work with hundreds of clients is this: *we sabotage ourselves from experiencing the very thing we want most.* Although we desperately want to be in a loving, lasting, long-term relationship, we are somehow blocking love from entering our lives. Discovering how we're doing this and breaking free of it is the conscious approach.

I opened this chapter with a quote from the mystic poet, Rumi, and it bears repeating:

Your task is not to seek love, but merely to seek and find all the barriers within yourself that you have built against it.

This is why the conventional approaches don't work. How can you attract lasting love if you have barriers built against that very thing? Think of it this way: The offensive linemen on a football team block the defenders from getting to the quarterback. Likewise, Rumi says you have "blockers" in your life, things that keep love from getting to you.

Let's look closer at what he's saying.

"Your task is not to seek love..." That phrase, alone, should make your head spin, for it's the exact opposite of everything you hear today! He's

saying not to bother with any of the conventional approaches that tell you how to find love. In fact, you should drop the entire search. Don't concern yourself with where to go, who you want, what to wear, how to approach and what to say. Instead, Rumi says, *"seek and find all the barriers within yourself"* that you have built against love. If you're going to seek for anything, seek the barriers.

Seek and find all the ways in which you're keeping yourself single.

However, that's easier said than done because the barriers are hidden from your awareness, which is why Rumi says you need to look for them. But you must, because they're destroying your ability to attract lasting love. Like the Wizard of Oz who was controlling everything from behind the curtain, so these barriers are "behind the curtain" of your awareness controlling your ability to attract and sustain a meaningful relationship.

Your task, then, is to seek, find and then break free of the barriers you've built against love and this book will show you how.

This is the approach that's changed my life and hundreds of my client's lives. If you drop the conventional approaches to finding a life partner and adopt this conscious approach, you too will attract lasting love.

The Overview

We are going to explore 7 barriers to love, and so the book has 7 sections. Each section has a number of chapters, so that each barrier is thoroughly discussed, and of course, dissolved.

There is a chance that some of the barriers will not be an issue in your life. Maybe there's only one that's keeping you single. I don't know. Only you can be the judge of that. What I do know is that you are single for a reason and if you're willing to be honest with yourself, this book will bring that reason to light and show you how to break free of it.

You'll notice that each chapter ends with what's called, "Attraction Factors." These are follow up questions and I *cannot* emphasize how important they are. The money is in the questions. Trust me. If you skip these, the book won't work for you.

Lastly, the 7 barriers are laid out in a specific order for a reason. They build on each other. If you skip ahead, you're sabotaging yourself. Stick to the order.

Now, here's a look at the 7 barriers:

THE 7 BARRIERS

#1: Choice—*Preparing for Something Real*
#2: Change—*Shifting Out of the Victim Mentality*
#3: Commitment—*The Secret to Attracting Lasting Love*
#4: Completion—*Making Space for Love to Appear*
#5: (de)Construction—*Releasing Your Relationship Persona*
#6: Competency —*Mastering Masculine/Feminine Dynamics*
#7: Creation—*The Art of Effortless Manifestation*

The first barrier, **CHOICE**, asks us to make some big picture choices in regards to 5 critical areas of our lives, all of which prepare us for something real. These are Monopoly game type choices, meaning, you cannot pass go or collect $200 unless you choose wisely.

The second barrier, **CHANGE**, is also preparatory in nature. Since this book is about changing your relationship status, it's important to understand how change works. This may not sound very sexy, but it's the whole ballgame. This is the shortest but most important section in the book.

The third barrier, **COMMITMENT**, is where the real inner work begins. Here we begin to see how certain fears hold us back from attracting lasting love. When my clients discover and dissolve these self-sabotaging fears, they often attract a great relationship immediately.

The fourth barrier, **COMPLETION**, will be the most challenging section in the book. You won't like it. I sure hated this part of my journey. But if you want to attract a great relationship, then you must be complete with former lovers. This section shows you why and how to do that.

The fifth barrier, **(de)CONSTRUCTION**, explains the bizarre experience of attracting the same kinds of partners and patterns over and over again. I call it the "Relationship Groundhog Day Syndrome" and it's caused by our relationship personas. It is critical to *de*construct these personas so that we can love from our authentic self. Your biggest "aha" moments may come in this section.

The sixth barrier, **COMPETENCY**, is where it really gets fun. When you've dissolved the first 5 barriers, you're now ready to attract your ideal partner and create a healthy relationship with them. But how does conscious attraction work? What is THE attraction factor? It's your Masculine or Feminine energy.

The seventh barrier, *CREATION*, is where I get into the nitty-gritty and talk about the actual things you can do to find your partner. Because you've let go of all your barriers to love, we can finally talk about conscious manifestation techniques.

A Final Word

Finally, the 7 Barriers you're about to face are very complex and deep subjects. This book is not like frolicking in a baby pool. It's more like a headfirst dive into the deep end—from the 10-meter platform. If you get stuck on any of the barriers because of the complexity of the subject matter, I encourage you to put the book down and send me an email so that we can make an appointment to talk. I'm sincere about this. I was not able to navigate these 7 Barriers on my own. My coach and guardian angel, Diana, walked with me every step of the way, and I would be honored to be "Clarence" for you. (But if not, that's ok. I've already got my wings.)

Attraction Factors

1. Put the 6 F-Words in order from the one you've used the most to the one you've used the least, and then give an example of how you used each one.

2. Which of the seven barriers do you think may be your biggest challenge and why?

3. Are you willing to make the conscious approach your only approach?

BARRIER ONE

CHOICE
Preparing for Something Real

To really lose yourself is like holding a gun to your head and pulling the trigger—it takes courage. Facing the truth means tying a bag over your head until you suffocate—it takes faith. You have to be brave to follow God's tracks into the unknown where so many new things overwhelm and panic you, but trust me and plunge the jeweled dagger into your heart. This is what it takes to lose yourself. There is no other path to God.

~ Hafiz

Running a marathon is not so much about the race itself as it is about the preparation. No matter how much you want to finish the race, unless you're adequately prepared for it, you never will.

It's that way in attracting lasting love. I know how much you want to meet, date, love, and maybe even marry your ideal partner, but unless you're adequately prepared for it, you never will.

So the first barrier to attracting lasting love is that we are unprepared to create something real. There are 5 critical choices that we have to make before we seek to find our life partner. Here are the choices:

Chapter 1:   Scarcity or Abundance?
Chapter 2:   Life Source or Life Partner?
Chapter 3:   Rigid or Adaptable?
Chapter 4:   Occupied or Available?
Chapter 5:   Shallow or Deep?

— 1 —

Scarcity or Abundance?

"It's raining men, Hallelujah, it's raining men."

~ The Weather Girls[6]

The first and most important issue to address as we embark upon the journey to consciously attract lasting love is to ask ourselves how we view the world. Do we believe there's enough, or do we believe in scarcity?[7] Is it "raining men" (or women), or is there a shortage of quality, available partners in the world? Which is it? Feast or famine, scarcity or abundance?

Nothing will sabotage our ability to attract lasting love more than a scarcity mentality and that's why we begin the book with it. Unless we choose abundance over scarcity, we'll keep ourselves single, *because our beliefs create our reality.*

Now, I'm well aware that, statistically, it's rare to find a good relationship after 40. My clients tell me all the time: All the good ones are taken or gay. My male clients say things like, "Women are all gold-diggers, ballbusters or riddled with baggage. There aren't any good women out there." My female clients often say, "Men are either married and lying about it, or they're players, mama's boys or looking for women half their age." On and on it goes. The viewpoint is that finding a quality partner is like looking for a needle in a haystack.

They try to convince me that scarcity is not just their opinion—it's actually the Truth, with a capital "T." It's reality. They actually get angry with me when I say it's just a story they're making up, a perspective they're projecting out into the world and then finding evidence for. "No," they say, "It's true. There are no good men (or women) out there."

That's when I get to say, "Do you know how old I was when I met my wife? 47. And I'm a pretty good guy. And she was a little bit older than me, and she's definitely a good woman. So...do you want to continue believing

---

[6] Enjoy. http://bit.ly/1rn1IL8

[7] "Scarcity" is one of the 7 commitments in my *Dating Manifesto*, found in Appendix I.

that your scarcity story is the absolute TRUTH?" The sad thing is they often do.

The Danger of Scarcity

Don't underestimate the power of a scarcity mentality. It causes six dangerous results.

1. **Stuck.** Our beliefs create reality, not the other way around. The world is a projection of our minds. When we believe in scarcity, we experience scarcity. And when we experience scarcity, it then strengthens our belief in scarcity. On and on it goes. We end up *stuck* in an endless, self-fulfilling loop.

2. **Sour.** A scarcity mindset creates a dark, negative energy in us. It *sours* our mood, saps our aliveness and closes our hearts. And sour people aren't very fun to be around, nor do they get many dates.

3. **Settle.** Quite simply, if there is not an abundance of quality, available partners, we'll *settle* for what we can get. But if we think it's "raining men" (or women), we'll wait for the right one.

4. **Stay.** If we believe in scarcity, then we're likely to *stay* in unfulfilling, distant, even unhealthy relationships, believing we can't do any better.

5. **Seek.** The most unattractive energy you can carry in the dating scene is desperate energy. Scarcity makes us *seek*. We come on too strong and try too hard.

6. **Spend.** Perhaps the most dangerous thing a scarcity mentality does is it causes us to *spend* too much energy obsessing on external issues, like where and how to find a partner, rather than on internal matters, like the 7 barriers.

The Choice

My guess is that we understand the significance of this barrier. The question is, how do we release the scarcity mindset and choose abundance? Well, it begins with admitting that this is an issue for us and that we want to let it go. Once we're willing to do that, then there are six steps to releasing the scarcity mindset.

1. **Select.** The first step is to *select* a name for our scarcity mindset. In a way, it's like a persona, and naming it puts a little distance be-

tween it and us. So come up with a fun name, something like, "Scarcity Suzy," or "Scarcity Sam."

2. **Script**. Next, create a script of the words, phrases and stories that Scarcity Suzy or Scarcity Sam uses. What does he or she say inside your head and also out loud to friends, family and co-workers? Put it all on paper.

3. **Shift**. One of the principles of conscious living is to realize that the opposite of our story could be as true, or truer than the story we're currently telling.[8] So, take your script and *shift* it by writing its opposite. For example, "There are no good men (or women) in my area," becomes "There is an abundance of good, quality men (or women) in my area." Do this for every word, phrase or story in your script.

4. **Speak**. Make the commitment to intentionally and verbally *speak* of abundance. Write affirmations and post them on your bathroom mirror or on your refrigerator. Say them out loud to yourself. When you're out with your friends, actually say, "Wow! This place is packed with a bunch of people who'd be great partners for me. I can't wait to meet them all."

5. **See**. I regularly encourage my clients to spend time in nature because if they really open their eyes and look at the world around them, they will *see* that the nature of reality is abundance. Do the birds worry about finding worms? Do trees fret about getting enough rain? Do grizzly bears agonize about the supply of salmon in the river? Go outside and witness abundance.

6. **Switch**. Finally, in a spirit of curiosity and wonder, *switch* the question from, "Where and how will I find the right partner?" to "What are my barriers to love and how can I release them?" In other words, switch from an external focus to an internal one.

One of my favorite actors is Jim Carrey. Back when he had nothing and was not yet famous, he wrote himself a check for 10 million dollars. It was for acting services rendered, and he post-dated it three years in the future, Thanksgiving, 1995. The check stayed in his wallet, folded and withering away, all but forgotten. Almost exactly three years later he was informed he was going to make 10 million dollars for *Dumb and Dumber*.[9]

---

[8] "Story" is one of the 7 commitments in my *Dating Manifesto*, found in Appendix I.

[9] See his discussion of this with Oprah here: http://bit.ly/TLLaxU

Jim Carrey did not have a scarcity mentality. He believed there was enough in the world for him, *even when there was no evidence of it in his present day experience.*

Are you committed to scarcity or abundance? Is it, or is it not, "raining men"?

Attraction Factors

1. Get a marriage certificate and put your name and the date of your wedding on it.

2. Spend time in nature this week and see if you can find evidence of lack and scarcity.

3. Every time you're out with friends, make a point of saying something that reveals an abundance mentality, *even if it doesn't feel true.* Notice how your friends react to such words and how it feels in your body.

— 2 —

Life Source or Life Partner?

"The purpose of a relationship is not to have another who might complete you, but to have another with whom you might share your completeness."

~ Neale Donald Walsch

Do you remember the 1996 movie, *Jerry Maguire*, starring Tom Cruise? I loved it. I really did. It was funny, sweet and romantic. It even had a couple of really conscious scenes in it. But it also had the "you complete me" scene[10] and that's why I say...

Jerry Maguire was full of shit!

If there is one thing I stand for in this world more than anything else it's that the "you complete me" mindset, sometimes known as "the soulmate syndrome,"[11] is the single most dangerous—and common—relationship perspective in the world today. It is THE root cause of drama and pain, and almost all of us have this disease, yet we don't even know it! That was certainly true in my life. Here's how I described it in my first book, *Relationship Addiction—A Memoir*:

> With the help of a relationship coach, I was able to discover the core issue that was responsible for *all* of my relationship pain. Although I had been in a bunch of relationships with very different women, all of the drama and heartache was coming from one single root issue, which was this: I was relying on the attention and the affection of my partner(s) to make me feel special, alive and whole. In other words, I saw a relationship as the means to alleviate my feelings of loneliness, to be the source of my happiness, to validate my masculinity and to secure my self-esteem.

---

10 Here's the scene: http://bit.ly/1rpAWSa

11 See chapter 8 in: *Relationship Addiction—A Memoir: How One Man "Sobered Up" from One of the World's Most Common Addictions and How You Can Too.*

Forgive me for using a corny, overdone cliché, but the truth was that I had an unconscious belief in a concept that the movie *Jerry Maguire* made famous: "You Complete Me."

Now, I loved that movie…however, if you asked me if the "You Complete Me" mindset was technically healthy and appropriate, I would have said flatly, "HELL NO!" My brain would have said that another person isn't responsible for my happiness. That's my job. And my brain would have also said that it's not my partner's job to alleviate my feelings of loneliness or to make me feel special or whole. But while my head might have said that, my life was saying something altogether different. In reality, I *was* relying on my partner(s) to meet those emotional needs.

So there it is. It took me about a year of coaching to finally see this. The core issue that was responsible for all of my relationship pain and drama was that I was relying on a partner's attention and affection to make me feel special, alive and whole.

And so are you.

Sorry to seem so presumptuous, but unless you've done an enormous amount of growth work you have "faith in love," meaning, you believe that finding the right relationship will *fix* a problem, *fill* a void, *find* an identity or *finish* a story. What I've learned is that all but the most enlightened beings among us are expecting their life partner's to be their Life Sources.[12] Let me put it this way:

Life partners make lousy life sources

One more quote from my first book:

"…if you are lonely and you think a relationship would fix that, or if you believe that a partner's love will make you feel better about yourself, or if you think you would be happier if you were in a committed relationship, those are signs of being hooked and addicted to love, as I define it here. The essence of relationship addiction is the *reliance* on a person to give you that which you cannot, or will not, give yourself. Drama is the guaranteed outcome of such external reliance, because when you feel that your

---

[12] "Source" is one of the 7 commitments in my *Dating Manifesto*, found in Appendix I.

partner's affection or attention is inadequate, "withdrawal" sets in and drama begins.

Any time we are unaware of, or disconnected from, our [Essence], the Ground of All Being, we invariably turn to *external* things to give us that which we *seem* to lack internally...

In other words, to look within is to find you *are* everything you need; to look without, in order to fulfill a *perceived* need...always leads to drama and suffering. *Relationship addiction is your ego's attempt to find itself in another person.*

The Choice

So, here's the principle we arrive at:

> *Before we think about attracting lasting love,*
> *we first need to break our addiction to love.*

This single issue, more than any other, was THE reason why my love life sucked for so long. It's the underlying cause of all your relationship drama and frustration too. If you don't believe me, then I ask you to trust me on this one. My love life is amazing because I faced this issue head on. I'm inviting you to look at this issue as I did, to put your full attention on it, and you do that by reading my first book.

Attraction Factors

1. Are you willing to read my first book, *Relationship Addiction—A Memoir*?

2. Do some honest, introspective work here. Why do you want a relationship in the first place? Don't fool yourself. What are you really after? Is it to **fix** a problem, **fill** a void, **find** an identity or **finish** a story?

3. This is a very challenging subject, one that's not easy to work through on your own. You'll notice that I had the help of a coach. Do you need that too?

— 3 —

Rigid or Adaptable?

"Men are born soft and supple; dead, they are stiff and hard...
Thus whoever is stiff and inflexible is a disciple of death.
Whoever is soft and yielding is a disciple of life."

~ Lao Tsu

The older we are, and the longer we've been single, the more we tend to be rigid, inflexible and set in our ways. This is one of the sneakiest barriers to attracting and growing a great relationship and it's rarely spoken about.

We get used to living life a certain way, don't we? We do what we want, when we want and how we want. Our living space is decorated and organized the way we want it. Our schedules, where we go, what we do, even how we spend our money, impacts no one but us. Frankly, this is one of the advantages to being single. We don't have to adapt, adjust or modify our lives in any way for what someone else wants, who they are and how they live.

What happens, then, when we attract a partner who's just as stubborn and set in their ways as we are? (And they will be.) No matter how compatible the two of you are, there's going to be a lot of significant differences.

The Choice

Are you rigid, inflexible and unyielding? This is another huge issue we have to face as we prepare for something real. We must let go of the scarcity mentality, we must let go of the "you complete me" mentality, and now, we must let go of the "it's my way or the highway" mentality.

Let's be perfectly clear about something. I am *not* saying that in order to be in a relationship you have to give up control of your life and become a doormat, nor am I talking about compromise, which is a lose/lose mentality. (With a bit of curiosity, a couple can always find win/win solutions.) So I'm not saying that a relationship means you lose yourself in some way, but I am saying you will have to take someone else into consideration. And if you've been single for a while, and especially if you're over 35, this won't be easy. You will be challenged to adapt in three primary ways: logistically, psychologically and energetically. Let's look at them one at a time.

Logistical Adaptation

When two stubborn people begin to blend their lives together, there's the possibility of turf wars. Each person is used to *their* structure, *their* way, *their* system and having complete control over everything.

For example, my wife and I have very different definitions of what clean is. Additionally, she buys lots of organic food and I think the whole organic thing is propaganda and a waste of money. Also, every few months she rearranges the furniture, pictures and plants in our home—for no reason, it seems, other than to drive me insane! And don't even get me started with how she loads the dishwasher. She'll run the damn thing without it being full. Who lives like that?

What if your future partner sleeps on *your* side of the bed or just has weird sleeping habits in general? What if they never throw anything away, or have more clothes and shoes than a mall? What if he wants a "man cave," or is a bit OCD, or wants control of the A/C? God, what if he's a morning person?

In other words, having a life partner is wonderful, *right up until the time you move in together!* How stubborn and set in your ways are you? Are you willing to adapt—logistically?

Psychological Adaptation

I think God has a strange and sick sense of humor because one of the divine laws of the universe is that opposites attract. Think about how cruel that is! While it is important that you share a few things in common with your life partner and that you're compatible in terms of your general lifestyle and relationship building blueprint, the person you attract is going to be your opposite in many, many ways.

My wife and I are perfectly compatible and yet we are total opposites when it comes to our psychology and personalities. For example, I'm a man and she's a woman. Hell, that's as incompatible as it gets!! I'm not trying to be funny. (Well, maybe a little.) Seriously, the Masculine and Feminine energies could not be more different. But it gets worse. Here's a short list of the ways in which my wife and I differ:

- I rarely speak to anyone in my family, other than my son. My wife, however, is on the phone all the time, intimately involved in the lives of her kids, her sisters, her mother, her nieces, her nephews and their kids. It exhausts me just thinking about it.

- I'm athletic and extremely competitive, my favorite channel being *ESPN*. She has zero interest in sports (not even the Super Bowl!) and doesn't have a competitive bone in her body. She likes *The Hallmark Channel*.
- I'm aggressive, she's easy-going. I'm a risk-taker, she's cautious. I'm impulsive, she's thoughtful. I'm a hare, she's a tortoise. I'm entrepreneurial, she's a team player.
- I'm a big picture guy, having not balanced my checkbook in decades. She's detail-oriented and has an Excel spreadsheet for everything.
- I like to be out in public, in front of a camera or on stage. She likes to stay in the background and not be seen.
- I like to get out of the house, she's a homebody.

You and your future partner may, or may not, be as different as I am from my wife, but make no mistake about it, your psychology and personalities will be different. Guaranteed. It's the Law of Opposites. The issue is, are you willing to adapt to them or will you rigidly think your way is "right" and then try to change them to be more like you? (By the way, that's a great way to ruin a relationship: tell them they're wrong and try to change them. *That'll keep you single.*)

Energetic Adaptation

Let's go deeper. This one's a bit more complicated.

In order to live an effective life as a single person, you have to regularly animate both your Masculine and Feminine sides. It doesn't matter what gender you are, you need both energies to be regularly operating in your life if you're going to function in the world in positive way.

We're going to get into a detailed discussion of Masculine/Feminine dynamics in Part 6, but for now, it's enough to know that the Masculine part of any human being is the directional energy within them. It's about where they're going and how they're going to get there. This is necessary in any person's life, man or woman. The Feminine part of any human being is the connection energy within them. It's about the flow of love in relationship. This is a necessary part of any person's life as well. The Masculine is about "go", the Feminine is about "flow". Again, to lead an effective life, we need both of these energies fully operational in our lives.

However, almost all of us are identified with one energy more than the other, meaning, one comes easier to us than the other does. It seems more natural, more like home. We're better at it, for lack of a better way to say it. Normally, but not always, women are more identified with Feminine energy, while men are more identified with Masculine energy.

A person identified with Feminine energy feels most alive, happy and fulfilled when they're able to give their Feminine, connection energy to an intimate partner. Likewise, a person identified with Masculine energy feels most alive, happy and fulfilled when they're able to give their Masculine, directional energy to an intimate partner.

Each person wants to give their native energy *as a gift* to the other, and yet, as single people, we've been animating both energies ourselves, possibly for years. We've had to because we're single.

Here's the question: Are we willing to relax our non-dominant energy and allow our partner to give us their gift, *to let them take over that role in our lives?*

If not, you will never attract lasting love.

Why would they want to be with you if you don't want what they desire to give? So, unless and until you're willing to adapt to, and receive, what they want to give, you'll stay single.

This means, if you're a woman, letting a man *direct* your life, and it means, if you're a man, letting a woman *connect* your life. You've been doing these things yourself, but a conscious relationship is one in which you choose a man or woman *who's worthy of such trust*, and allow them to give you that which you'd rather not give yourself.

Are you willing to adapt—energetically?

Attraction Factors
1. Make a list of the ways in which you might be hard to live with. If you need help with this, ask your friends, children, or if you're really brave, ask your Ex!

2. Knowing that opposite personalities attract, make a list of the personality traits that would be the most difficult for you to accept and adapt to.

3. Describe a specific situation where it might be challenging to allow your future partner the space to express their Masculine or Feminine presence in your new life together.

— 4 —

Occupied or Available?

"I'm making space for the unknown future to fill up my life with yet-to-come surprises."

~ Elizabeth Gilbert

Quality single people lead busy, full lives. I'm sure that's true of you. Between your career, family, possibly children, friends, hobbies, managing your household and other interests, you don't have large blocks of free time in your schedule. (Hell, you probably struggle to find time to read this book!)

Because nobody wants to sit around, feeling lonely, with nothing to do, we keep ourselves busy with people, activities and commitments. That's totally understandable. But an intimate relationship takes up a lot of time and space in our lives.

The Choice

So here's an important issue that we rarely talk about: Is there room in your life for a relationship? Seriously. I know that sounds crazy, but since a relationship takes a serious commitment of time and energy, is there space available for him or her, or is your life so occupied and busy that you really don't know where a partner would fit?

Imagine walking into a hotel lobby looking for a place to stay for the night. You walk up to the counter and the attendant says, "sorry, we're completely full. There's no room for you." Likewise, suppose a quality person walks into the lobby of your life and says, "I'd like to stay here with you." Is there room for them or would you have to turn them away?

"I'd love to go out with you. Let me look at my schedule. Humm…I've got an hour open two weeks from Thursday. How's that?" I think I might walk away and find another hotel. There's no room in the Inn.

My wife's sister is a single, attractive woman with a good job. She'd be a great partner for someone. I don't think she's interested in finding someone, but if she were, I don't know where a guy would fit. She has both of her daughters and their families living with her, a total of 8 people—in a smallish home! Additionally, she's so emotionally wrapped up in her kids' lives and caring for her other family members, that there is absolutely no way she could even date, much less seriously engage with a man.

That's sort of an extreme example, but I think you see my point. Your life can be so consumed with work, or so wrapped up in the lives of others, or so obsessed with hobbies or other interests, that you're literally undateable.

Now, does this mean you need to quit your job, ignore your family and sit home alone, twiddling your thumbs, so that there's space for a partner in your life? Obviously not. You do, however, need to audit your life and consider where your ideal partner is going to fit. Remember, there's only 24 hours in a day and if all the hours are taken, something has to give. You can't put more water into a glass that's already full.

Let's say you meet someone *this week*. That could happen. Look at the way my wife and I met. It was totally random and unexpected. But we hit it off immediately, and had I not been going out of town the following day, I would have wanted to see her again very soon. But what if she was like her sister, committed to a lifestyle in which I couldn't fit? Well, she would have missed out on an amazing man! (Smile.)

However, don't overcomplicate this. Perhaps your future partner will share many of your interests and maybe your careers will mesh and your families will blend well together. Maybe you won't have to cut much out. I don't know. All I'm saying is that this is an issue that needs some attention and some difficult choices might need to be made.

So, the question is, are you occupied or available?

Attraction Factors

1. If attracting a lasting, intimate relationship is a priority, what aspect of your lifestyle are you planning to restructure—at a moment's notice—in order to make space for love?

— 5 —

Shallow or Deep?

"When you embark on creating a conscious, loving relationship, you need to consider depth—your own depth and the depth of the person you want— because some day the pecs will deflate and the belly dancer contours will lose their definition."

~ Dr. Gay Hendricks

The final issue to address, as we complete our discussion of the first barrier, is to choose which impulse within us is going to dictate who we want as our life partner. Are we going to follow the impulses of our shallow-self or of our deeper-self? In other words, are we going to align with Ego or Essence? They have two very different agendas.

When we get to *Barrier 7: Creation*, we will talk about the proverbial list of qualities we want in a partner. Unfortunately, "the list" is usually thought to be the be-all, end-all of attraction, yet it's only a very small part of the process. *Who we are is way more important than who we want.* But, having said that, the list is important and we will get to it.

When we do, who is going to be in charge of what goes on it and what doesn't? Ego or Essence? Ego is the fear-driven, image conscious and shallow part of us, while Essence is our deeper, authentic and fearless self. At the risk of over generalizing, when the male ego is running the show, a woman's age is at the top of his list. She must be younger than him, and usually significantly younger. And, it seems, the older a man gets, the more he wants a younger woman. What's behind a man's obsession with a woman's age?

Well, on the surface, men say that younger women are more energetic, sexually active, and healthier. And frankly, ladies, this is feedback you need to hear. Age does not have to diminish your Feminine radiance. While you can't control your age, you can control your aliveness, sexuality and fitness. However, the real reason, in my view, why men want younger women is that they enhance their image, especially among their male peers, and younger women also distract men from the fear of their own mortality (this goes for "Cougars," too). Younger partners make us look better and feel younger. This is pure Ego—enhancing image, fearing death.

What about the female Ego? (There is such a thing, you know.) Well, if the male Ego prioritizes a woman's age over everything else, a woman's Ego prioritizes a man's finances over everything else. What's behind this?

Well, on the surface, women will say the size of a man's bank account reflects his general character and trustworthiness. And frankly, this is good feedback for men too. If men aren't financially stable, why would women want to be a part of their lives? But, just as a man's desire for a younger woman is not really about her vitality, sexuality and fitness, so a woman's desire for a rich guy isn't about his character and trustworthiness. It's about her Ego too. A man with money can enhance her image, especially among her female peers, because he can give her nice things, and his money can make her feel safe and secure, diminishing the fear of her own mortality.

Now, what does all this mean? Am I saying men should only pursue women who are their age and that women shouldn't be concerned if a man has a job or not? Of course not. All I'm saying is that if a woman's age and a man's finances are your priorities, and appear at the TOP of your list, I think you'll end up regretting it. Depth is what really matters and what leads to lasting love.

The Choice

Are we going to focus on matters of depth—ours and theirs, qualities like integrity, purpose, empathy, spirituality and compatibility, or are we going to follow our more shallow impulses and prioritize age and financial status over everything else?

Can you have both? Sure. But if you met a really amazing person of depth, someone with whom you clicked on every level, are you going to kick them to the curb because of their age, or because their income was that of a school teacher?

About 5 months after I had met my wife, MaryMargaret, I was telling my coach how much I liked her, how good we seemed together, and yet she could hear the hesitancy in my voice. I wasn't sure she was "the one." Finally, I said, "Well, she's a couple of years older than me." The phone went silent. Then, "Are you telling me that this woman is everything you want, she's beautiful, spiritual, and you love being around her, and yet you're considering breaking it off with her, solely because she's a bit older than you?" Sheepishly, I admitted, "Ya." She yelled, "Grow the fuck up, Roy! That's just ego bullshit!"

She was right. It was. There was this little voice in the back of my head wondering what my friends would think of me if I were with an older woman. And I was approaching 50 at the time and a younger woman would help me forget that too.

As we move forward, who's going to run the show—Ego or Essence?

Attraction Factors

1. If you are seeking a partner who is significantly younger than you are or one who has financial abundance, write a short paragraph describing what that is really about.

2. What do you think are the types of qualities that really matter in the long run? Are you willing to prioritize them in your search for a life partner?

3. Knowing that both men and women want a partner who takes care of their physical and financial lives, which area do you need to work on, and what—*exactly*—are you going to do about it?

BARRIER TWO

CHANGE
Shifting Out of the Victim Mentality

Are you willing to be sponged out, erased, cancelled? Are you willing to be made nothing, dipped into oblivion? If not, you will never really change.

~ D.H. Lawrence

This second section of the book is the foundation of the entire conscious approach, better known as Rumi's Way. Everything we talk about from here on will be built upon the ideas and principles presented in the next two chapters, so really do your best to understand what I'm saying.

A victim state of consciousness is the second barrier to attracting lasting love. Feeling "at the effect of" makes changing your relationship status impossible.

As crazy as this sounds, I'm inviting you to open up to the possibility that you are living with a victim state of consciousness (even if you don't know how) and that it's keeping you single. Just a little openness and curiosity is all I'm asking for.

Here's how this section breaks down:

— 6 —

Whose Movie Are You In?

"Your vision will become clear only when you can look inside your own heart. Who looks outside, dreams; who looks inside awakens."

~ Carl Jung

Imagine that you're in a blockbuster Hollywood movie, but playing just a bit part. You don't have the leading role or even a supporting one. You're just an actor in somebody else's movie. Obviously, you aren't producing, directing, writing or casting the movie. In fact, you don't have a say over anything. You don't get to choose your lines, you don't get to decide who's in a scene with you and you don't get to decide on the plot or what happens. It's *not your movie*. You're just acting in someone else's movie.

Now, imagine a different scenario. It's the same Hollywood blockbuster, but instead of playing a bit part in someone else's movie, having no control or say over anything—*this time it's your movie*.

This time, you're the star, playing the leading role, but it goes beyond even that. You're also the producer, director, writer and the casting agent. In other words, you're in charge of everything. You've decided on the plot and its twists because you wrote the script. You are directing every aspect of the movie. As a matter of fact, you've gone out and personally hand-selected all the actors in the movie, especially your co-stars. You've determined their roles, told them when to appear in your movie and for how long, and you've even told them exactly what to do and what to say. In other words, you are in control of absolutely everything. *It's your movie.*

Life Is Like A Movie
What is your view of life and your role in it? Are you in somebody else's movie, with no power or control over anything, or is this your movie? Are you "at the effect of" someone else's script, casting and direction, or did you *choose* everyone in your movie, assign them their roles and give them their lines? Have you *chosen* your life's plot, with all its twists and turns, or has it all just happened to you?

Again, I ask, what is your view of life and your role in it? This is THE core question of the conscious approach.

Is life happening "to you" or "by you"?

How you answer this question will determine if your love life changes or stays stuck in repeating patterns of frustration and pain.

You have the power to choose which one of these two perspectives will govern your life. That's the bottom line—it's your choice. You can choose to see yourself as a victim, having no control over the script, or you can choose to see yourself as the creator of your experience, the one who is and has been writing the script.

I am suggesting that you're not a victim, that life is not happening "to you" but "by you," or because of you. This is not somebody else's movie. This is your movie and you're in charge of everything and everyone in it—past, present and future. But this is my choice to see life this way. How are you choosing to see life and your role in it?

Breathe!

Is your head spinning? I know mine was when I first heard this. The implications of it are absolutely staggering. For example, if it's your movie, how could you ever blame anyone for anything? How could you even complain about something? And would there ever be a need to forgive anyone? Not if you're choosing the plot, picking the actors and writing their lines. Perhaps only self-forgiveness would be necessary for writing pain into your own life!

Do you see how mind-blowing this is?

In fact, it's so radical that I'm concerned I might lose you right here, that you might put this book down and walk away. When my coach first explained the victim/creator dynamic to me, I not only thought she was out of her mind, but I came very close to bailing on the whole inward journey, including the conscious approach to life and love. But I stuck with it, probably because I recognized that all the conventional approaches to life and love weren't working. (Desperation does have its privileges.)

As I look back, I went through 6 distinct stages on the way to embracing the perspective that I'm not a victim (and that no one is). Here's what I experienced; perhaps this will help you hang in there.

1. **Defiance**. At first, I was outraged and defiant. *How dare you say I chose the things that have happened to me and the way people have treated me!*
2. **Disagree**. Then I softened a bit, but I still disagreed. *"This is Bullshit. There's no way this is true."*
3. **Debate**. The third stage was the most dangerous. *"What about people who were abused as children or were abandoned by alcoholic parents? Did they choose that?* We're really not talking about that sort of thing. As I look back on my debating phase, I realize it was a smoke screen to keep me from having to take responsibility for my life. Don't fall into the trap of trying to make sense out of this for everyone else. Just be curious about how you're creating your experience.
4. **Dazed**. When I dropped the "Johnnie Cochran" debating persona, I began to feel stunned, confused and dazed. *How could I...? Why would I...? Are you saying that...? Do you mean that...?*
5. **Depressed**. When I began to see how the 7 barriers had been sabotaging my love life, I became depressed. I couldn't believe what I had been doing to myself! It knocked the wind out of me.
6. **Delighted**. But my depression turned into delight when I realized that if I was writing the script, I could *rewrite* the script. The conscious approach is ultimately an empowering approach, because life is not happening "to you," it's happening "by you." If you choose to see yourself as the creator, then possibility, aliveness and joy will surge in your body.

The sole purpose of this chapter is to merely introduce the victim/creator dynamic and to see if you're willing to explore it in your life. I'm not expecting you to fully own it yet. It took me a while to work through the 6 stages, and it might take time for you too. That's fine. But if you're open and willing to explore, which we'll do in the next chapter, that's enough for now.

Attraction Factors
1. What's your reaction to the victim/creator dynamic and which D-word (defiant, disagree, debate, dazed, depressed, delight) best captures your current feelings?

— 7 —

Shifting from Victim to Creator Consciousness

"Some people say there's a woman to blame,
but I know, it's my own damn fault."

~ Jimmy Buffett

Many years ago I was a golf instructor. Every lesson would follow the same basic 3-step format. First, I'd video the player's swing before any changes were made. It was important that the player understand what they were doing wrong. Many times they'd be amazed when they saw their swing. *"I never knew I was doing that!"* they would say. The second step was to show them the correct way to swing the club, and then the third step was to go out to the practice tee and work on the changes, making the shift from the old swing to the new one.

Well, changing our relationship status is sort of like that. This chapter will take you through the same three steps. First, I want to show you your current "relationship swing." The "video" will show that the root of the problem is the victim mentality, and when you see it, you might say, *"I never knew I was doing that!"* Secondly, I'll show you a much better way to "swing," which is the creator mindset. Lastly, we'll talk about how to "change your swing," shifting from the old victim mentality to the new creator mentality, which is essential to attract lasting love.

Step One: Own Your Victim Consciousness

The best way to identify victim consciousness in your life is to ask yourself one simple question: *Why am I single?* (I encourage you to take a moment and write your reason in your notebook or Word doc.) If the reason you give is about anything "out there," rather than some known or unknown barrier within you, you're seeing yourself as a victim. Something is happening "to you."

The answer that sets the stage for insight and breakthrough is, "I don't know, but there must be something I'm doing, something I'm unaware of—

maybe I'm afraid of something or maybe it's something else. I don't know, but I'm really curious to learn about myself."

Notice the difference in where the attention is focused. The victim feels powerless and "at the effect of" outside forces, while the creator looks inward. How often do you hear things like this run through your mind or come out of your mouth?

- All the good ones are taken or gay.
- Men just want one thing and since I won't do that right away, no one will date me.
- If you don't have money, women won't give you the time of day.
- I just haven't met the right one yet.
- I don't know where or how to meet people.
- I'm too shy and introverted.
- The dating scene is filled with losers, liars and lunatics.
- I don't have good communication skills. I never know what to say.
- I won't have sex before marriage and that makes it hard to find someone.
- I don't know how to flirt and that makes it so hard to meet anyone.
- There aren't any quality people in the area in which I live.
- I'm too direct and no one likes that.
- I intimidate men.
- I'm too independent and self-sufficient.
- I've been married too many times. It scares people.
- I've never been married. It scares people.
- I'm not attractive enough.
- I'm too attractive. Men never approach me because they think I'm either in a relationship or that I'm out of their league.
- I refuse to go to bars or date online, so I can't meet anyone.
- I'm too picky.
- I'm too driven and focused on my career.
- I'm too short, too tall, too fat, too thin, too old, too young.
- Nobody wants a partner who has young kids (or kids like mine).
- My work and travel schedule holds me back.
- I'm not the nurturing type, which is what men want.
- I have health issues that turn people off.
- My personality is too quirky and different.
- I have too much emotional baggage from my past.
- I'm taking care of my parents. My life is just too complicated.

The dangerous thing about these victim statements (and the list could be much longer) is that nothing will change if we believe we're "at the effect of" some issue or circumstance over which we have no control.

Truth time. Be honest. Which one of those bullet points has been your reason for being single? Maybe you've got one that's not on the list. Either way, change begins by owning the victim mentality.

Step Two: Claim Your Creator Consciousness

The essence of the creator mentality is the understanding that *it's our movie*, that we are 100% responsible for our experience. Jimmy Buffett said it perfectly: "...some people say there's a woman to blame, *but I know, it's my own damn fault.*"[13]

Instead of blaming or finger pointing, you make the choice to simply claim responsibility. "I created the problem, so I can solve it," is the way the creator speaks. Nothing happens "to me," it happens "by me." The victim says, "Why is this happening to me?" The creator says, "How am I doing this to myself?"

This is a huge shift and it's not an easy one to make. It takes incredible courage and curiosity to open up to how we are somehow responsible for the condition of our love lives, especially when it *really* looks like one or more of those bullets points is true, and ruining our chances at attracting lasting love.

Step Three: Make The Shift

Now let's talk about how to shift out of the victim mentality, for, as long as we continue to embrace it, we'll stay stuck attracting the same kinds of partners, patterns, problems and pain. There are two primary shift moves and we've hinted at them already: responsibility and curiosity.[14]

The first is the willingness to claim responsibility for the condition of your love life. There's no magic here. You simply stop blaming and start claiming. "I created the problem, so I can solve it." You dismiss whatever reason you thought was responsible for keeping you single, and say instead, "I am doing *something* to sabotage myself, though I have no idea what that is."

Immediately curiosity and wonder are activated. This is the second shift move. A still, quiet presence arises and we begin to wonder: "Hummm...I

---

[13] Enjoy. http://bit.ly/ZLaNSs

[14] "Responsibility" and "curiosity" are the first two commitments in the *Dating Manifesto*, found in Appendix I.

wonder what that *something* is? Hummm…I wonder what I'm not seeing? Hummm…I wonder what barriers I have to love?" *Once we own that somehow we're responsible for the results we're experiencing, then the issue becomes, how am I creating this?*

Incredible things start to happen the moment we drop our convictions as to why we're single and become curious about the real reasons instead. Dr. Gay Hendricks writes,

> "The path of conscious living is paved with stepping-stones of wonder. Your wonder comes alive the moment you shift from conviction to curiosity. The wondering sojourner reaps a singular reward given only to those who keep their curiosity alive: pure, raw, unfiltered experience. One moment the raw experience may be blissful, the next moment unbearably painful or unfathomably confusing, but it is always genuine, direct and all yours."

Wonder Questions

Change begins the moment we shift from believing we're "at the effect of" some outside force and choose instead to be curious about how we are responsible for our experience. This is so much easier said than done. But if you're willing to be curious, amazing insights will come your way in the chapters that follow. Here are a few examples of wonder questions. Playfully pondering them will lead to incredible breakthroughs:

- How am I requiring my love life to be exactly as it is?
- How am I inviting this dating experience or pattern into my life?
- What are my barriers to love and intimacy?
- How do I push people away?
- What am I doing to attract this into my life?
- What attitude, persona, belief or energy is creating this result?
- What am I doing to sabotage my love life?
- How am I responsible for this situation?
- What can I learn about myself from this pattern in my life?
- I wonder how or why I'm keeping myself single. Hummm….

The sole purpose of this chapter has been to see if you'd be willing to drop whatever reason you think you're single and simply open up, in deep curiosity and wonder, to what the real reason might be. If you are, then you're ready to begin Part 3 of this book.

Attraction Factors

1. If you haven't recorded your reason(s) for being single in your notebook or Word doc, do it now. (In the future, when you've attracted a great relationship and proven your story to be a bunch of baloney, it will be fun to look back on it.)

2. Are you willing to become deeply curious about the real reason(s) you've been unable to attract and create lasting love?

3. Which wonder question caught your attention the most, and why?

4. Chances are high that an insight as to why you're single has already come into your awareness. Write it down in your notebook or in a Word doc.

BARRIER THREE

COMMITMENT
The Secret to Attracting Lasting Love

"The moment you understand that you're committed to things being the way they are now, you unleash a powerful force that will give you a rocket ride to your new commitment."

~ Dr. Gay Hendricks

I'm always skeptical when someone claims to have found "the secret" to something. It sounds too simplistic and I'm immediately turned off. However, as outrageous as this sounds, there is a secret to attracting lasting love and this section of the book is going to explain it.

On some unconscious level, you're fighting yourself. There's a commitment against the very thing you say you want most. But when you discover and dissolve this commitment, which is the third barrier to attracting lasting love, you will probably quickly attract your ideal partner, as many of my clients have. Take your time with the ideas presented in the next three chapters, for your love life literally depends on it.

Here's how this section breaks down:

Chapter 8:   The *Real* Reason You're Still Single
Chapter 9:   The Fear of Rejection
Chapter 10: The Fear of Engulfment

The *REAL* Reason You're Still Single

"The moment you realize that the way it is right now is the way you want it (usually on some unconscious level), you unleash a powerful force that will carry you to a new positive commitment that has nothing—repeat nothing!—to do with the past."

~ Dr. Gay Hendricks

You and I are best friends and today is a very special day. We're going on an incredible road trip together. You've been looking forward to this trip for as long as I can remember. It's all you talk about, which is sort of annoying, but it's okay because I know that it's more than a goal of yours. This is a bucket list item! Some people want to climb Mt. Everest; you want to go on this road trip. This is a big deal to you, a total life intention of yours. You've been reading books on our destination, visualizing and feeling it, planning, preparing, even praying about this trip. Simply put, I know that your life wouldn't feel complete without this trip. And because of that, I'm honored that you've asked me to join you.

And today's the day.

The car is gassed up and packed, we've got plenty of snacks, our iPod's are loaded with our favorite music and you even had the car checked out and tuned up. We're ready to rock and roll.

When you get behind the wheel, the car starts up beautifully and purrs like a kitten. Looking over at me with wide-eyed excitement, you say, "Ready?" I just smile. You put the car in drive, hit the gas...and the car jerks, but doesn't move!

"What the hell?" you say, reaching down to make sure it's not accidently in neutral. It's not. You hit the gas harder and the engine roars. The car shakes, but still won't move. Nothing. Not an inch.

Your facial expression has gone from excited to confused and angry. You go on a rant: "Roy, I really want to go on this trip! You know how much I want this, right? I mean, it's all I've been talking about. This trip has been my life's intention for years. Why is this happening? Why are we not moving? Why can't I get to my intended destination?

You're looking at me for answers. Tears are beginning to well up in your eyes because you're so disappointed, but I'm smiling, even laughing a bit.

"What the hell's so funny?" you yell. "How can you laugh when I'm losing my mind? We're ready to go, I've started the car, it's in "drive," I'm pushing the gas pedal and the damn car isn't moving. And all you're doing is laughing."

"Are you done" I say, just staring at you. "Yes."

"You've got your foot on the brake, dumbass."

Hidden Resistance

The *real* reason you're still single is that you have your foot on the brake (but you're not a dumbass).

I know you have a very strong intention to attract lasting love. It probably is a bucket list item for you. You *are*, in fact, reading a book on how to do it, and you probably know all about the Law of Attraction, visualizing and feeling the relationship you want, blah, blah, blah. And perhaps you've even prayed for it. So, I know your life won't feel complete if you don't experience a great relationship. All that is to say, I'm not disputing that your foot *is* on the "gas pedal." It definitely is. Attracting lasting love is your intention.

And it doesn't matter one single bit.

You can press the pedal all the way to the floor but nothing is going to happen because your other foot is on the brake. In other words, no matter how strong your intention is, underneath it is an even stronger commitment to staying single. For some reason, you do *NOT* want to be in a great relationship. How do I know that?

Because you're not.

Remember, you're not a victim, you're a creator. This is *your* movie and you've written the script. Your life is a reflection of your deepest commitments, whether you're conscious of them or not. Being single is not happening "to you," it's happening "by you." And for some reason, you must want to be single—because—well, you're single! (I'm committed to writing this book. How do I know that? Because I'm writing this book!) The fact of the matter is:

***You have a hidden, unconscious resistance to a relationship
and it's stronger than any intention you might have.***

Of the 7 barriers we're addressing in this book, the Commitment Barrier is by far the sneakiest, most powerful one of them all. You have one foot on the gas and the other on the brake—*and you don't know it.* And nothing will happen in your love life, it won't go anywhere, until this unconscious resistance/barrier is brought up into the light and dealt with.

The good news is, though, that while this is the sneakiest and most powerful barrier, it's the easiest one to release. It's a simple 3-step process: *Claim, Wonder, Listen.*

Claim, Wonder, Listen

Taking your foot off the brake begins by claiming responsibility for your current relationship status. It would sound something like this: "I am single right now, and for some unknown reason, I want to be. I'm sure of it and I *claim* responsibility for it. I'm not a victim. For some reason, I want to be single. I'm doing this to myself."

The moment you claim responsibility, you'll immediately begin to *wonder*, "How am I doing this to myself? Why am I resisting the very thing I want most?" Then you simply sit quietly in stillness, and *listen*. The answer will come—usually in a matter of seconds.

Sacred Space

Let's do this right now. I'm assuming you're willing to claim full responsibility for being single, that you've dropped the victim mentality completely, believing that somehow you've got your foot on the brake. With that being true, sit quietly with each of the following questions. Take them one at a time and don't rush. Say each one out loud, then close your eyes, sit quietly and listen. Bring a sense of sacredness to this. You're walking on holy ground, about to notice the *real* reason why you're single.

- What is the benefit of being single?
- What is the payoff or advantage of not being in a relationship?
- What do you fear you'd lose if you were in a relationship?
- What do you believe you'd have to give up to be in a relationship?
- What do you fear could happen if you were in a relationship?
- What is the downside of being in a relationship?

Attraction Factors

1. Why do you have your foot on the brake? In other words, why do you want to be single?

9

The Fear of Rejection

"If I had a prayer, it would be:
God, spare me from the desire for love, approval or appreciation. Amen."

~ Byron Katie

Gail was a smart, successful businesswoman in her early 40's. By anyone's standards, she was quite beautiful, yet with all she had going for her, she had never been married. In fact, she had never been in a meaningful, long-term relationship at all. She dated quite frequently, of course, but nothing ever went anywhere. She came to me confused and frustrated with this pattern, wanting to learn how to create a deep, lasting relationship with a great guy.

During one of our sessions, Gail was giving me some back-story on her life and casually mentioned that her parents divorced when she was 14. I asked what that was like. She said, "Oh, it was pretty awful. It was an ugly divorce. I remember telling myself back then that I would never let that happen to me." She started to go on with her life story and I interrupted her.

"Hold on, Gail. Back up a minute. Don't you think you made a commitment, back when you were 14, to never let a man get close to you?" She didn't know what I meant so I went on. "The best way to ensure that you never go through a messy, ugly divorce is to never have a relationship in the first place, don't you think?" Stunned silence. In that moment, she realized that her fear of a divorce, which is essentially the fear of rejection, had been keeping her single her entire life. She had her foot on the brake, yet didn't know it.

Wonder Questions

The benefit of wonder questions, like those I listed in the previous chapter, is that they can lead to profound "aha" moments, similar to what Gail experienced. Once we identified Gail's unconscious commitment to staying single, everything changed. She released her fear of rejection and loss, and quickly met someone and they've been together for over 2 years now.

When you answered those wonder questions, did you notice a particular theme? Were your answers all sort of saying the same thing? My guess is they were. As I've worked with clients on this commitment barrier, I've found that even though there are dozens of different ways to answer those questions, the answers usually fall into two broad, general categories: the fear of *rejection* or the fear of *engulfment*.

Being betrayed, played, abandoned, deceived, dumped or divorced, would fall in the "fear of rejection" category. It's the fear of being hurt, or the fear of loss. Conversely, the fear of being smothered, suffocated, tied down, taken advantage of, dominated, swallowed up, or "losing yourself in a relationship," would fall in the "fear of engulfment" category. It's the fear of being controlled or the loss of freedom.

Take a look at your answers. Don't they fall into one of those two categories? If you look closely, you'll see that they do.[15]

The reason you've got your foot on the brake, and therefore want to be single, is because you either fear being hurt or you fear being controlled. It's as simple as that.

But like Gail, when you take your foot off the brake by releasing whichever fear is keeping you single, your love life will accelerate like a racecar. *One of these two fears is probably the only thing keeping you out of a relationship.* This chapter is devoted to releasing the fear of rejection and the next chapter is about the fear of engulfment.

Rejection

The possibility of being rejected and hurt is really powerful and quite scary. Most of us want to avoid it like the plague. If this fear is allowed to run around in the background of our awareness unexamined, as it was for Gail, we will keep ourselves out of a relationship. We will sabotage ourselves somewhere in the dating process because there's just too much at stake.

Before I was married, I remember going to singles' clubs and not saying a word to anyone. I just stood there—for hours—terrified of being "shot

---

[15] It is possible to have both fears, but in my experience, most people fear one more than the other.

down." I could not bring myself to walk up to a woman and simply say, "Hello, my name is Roy." I thought that if a woman gave me the cold shoulder I would die. How can you get into a relationship if you're afraid to approach someone?

What about you? How do you protect yourself from the possibility of being hurt or rejected? How does it manifest in your life? As I said, this is a sneaky dynamic, so here are more wonder questions that may help you see how this fear is keeping you single:

- You've always prided yourself on being picky because you have high standards. But is it really about your standards, or is being picky an unconscious way to stay out of a relationship and keep from getting hurt? Hmmm…

- Is your pattern of choosing unavailable partners really just bad luck, or do you unconsciously choose them *because* they're unavailable, knowing there's no real risk of getting hurt? Hmmm…(Who's really unavailable—them or you?)

- Doing background checks, Google and social media searches, is that a legitimate concern for your safety or are you trying to find reasons to stay out of a relationship? Hmmm…

- When you break it off with someone who is "moving too fast," or feels "needy and clingy," are you really concerned about their emotional health, or does the clear opportunity for intimacy scare the shit out of you? Hmmm…

- Is being a shy, reserved, quiet, introverted and private person your personality, or is it a way to keep people at arm's length, so there's no risk of being hurt? Hmmm…

- Is your independence and self-sufficiency a true expression of your essence, or is it a defense mechanism, a wall, intended to keep you from being hurt? Hmmm…

- Your devotion to your kids, friends, family and hobbies, are those time commitments an authentic expression of your heart's deepest desire, or are they smoke screens, hiding the fact that you're really afraid of being hurt? Hmmm…

Releasing the Fear of Rejection

Once you know how the fear of being hurt and rejected is keeping you single, your task is then to look closely at this dynamic and understand why it has such power in your life. Seeing how fear works will allow you to release it and open your heart to love. And while a whole book could be written on this subject, I'll simply share a couple of insights that have made a huge difference in my clients' lives and in mine.[16]

The first thing to notice is that when we experience rejection in the form of getting the cold shoulder, not being asked for our phone number or even when we're deceived, dumped or divorced, it's not the rejection *event* itself we fear as much as what the event *means about us*. We interpret those events to mean something about who we are. It says something about us. That's where the pain and fear comes from.

For example, if I approach a woman and get the cold shoulder, yes, a rejection happened, but there's nothing inherently painful in that event *unless I make it mean something about me*. If I interpret her disinterest to mean I'm unattractive and nobody will ever want me (that is how I interpreted it), if I make it mean something about me and my future, now I've been **R**ejected, with a big, fat capital "R."

Stories of Deficiency

This brings up a critical insight into the human condition: We all have deeply held, and rarely recognized, core stories of deficiency or inadequacy about who we are. Deep down we carry stories like, "I'm unlovable," "I'm unwanted," "I'm unattractive," "I'm not good enough," "I'm unworthy," "I'm abandoned," and so on.

Without these kinds of stories, a rejection event might be unpleasant or even disappointing, but it wouldn't be a big deal. It wouldn't *mean* anything beyond the simple fact that they're not interested in us. That's all. It doesn't mean anything about us, or what our future holds, *unless we already have that story inside of us.*

Here's a crazy example, but it makes the point.

If someone rejects you, saying, "you're a green frog and I don't want to go out with you," my guess is you might be confused by that, but you wouldn't feel hurt or rejected, would you? Why not? They have, in fact, rejected you. Why doesn't it hurt? *Because you don't hold the story that you're Kermit!, that's why.* The rejection isn't taken personally because you don't have a personal, core story of being *Kermit*. It's just their opinion, and nothing more.

But what if someone says, "You're ugly and I don't want to go out with you"? If you hear that any differently than someone calling you a "green

---

[16] If this issue is THE barrier keeping you single, consider working directly with me. It can be challenging to unwind on your own.

frog," it's because *you think you're ugly and unattractive.* You take it personally because of your own deeply held core story of deficiency. "Green frog" and "ugly" are just someone else's opinions. They don't have the power to hurt you unless you already have a story that you're *Kermit* or ugly.

If someone told *Angelina Jolie* that she was ugly and that they didn't want to go out with her, would she be crushed and feel rejected? Probably not. Why? Because she doesn't think she's ugly and unattractive.[17]

Whatever form of rejection you fear—being dismissed, disliked, deceived, dumped or divorced, none of it is about you. It's not personal. It has nothing to do with who you are and what your future holds—*unless you make it mean that.*

However, you can recognize your core stories of deficiency and inadequacy and see how silly they are. You can choose to love and value yourself. You can own your worth, whether you look like Angelina (or Brad) or not. Our core stories are meaningless thoughts in our heads and there's nothing real or solid about them.

Perhaps you had a crush on someone back in high school and they wouldn't give you the time of day. Perhaps the love of your life cheated on you. Perhaps no one is responding to your online profile. Perhaps your fiancée dumped you, as mine did. Perhaps your father ignored you. None of it means anything about who you are and what your future holds—unless *you* make it mean something. Whatever someone says or does in relation to you is just their opinion and nothing more.

It's Not Personal
Don Miguel Ruiz wrote an excellent book called, *The Four Agreements*, and his second agreement is, "Don't take anything personally." He writes:

> "You take it personally because you agree with whatever was said...Even when a situation seems so personal, even if others insult you directly, it has nothing to do with you...If someone says, "Hey, you look fat," don't take it personally, because the truth is that this person is dealing with his or her own feelings, beliefs and opinions."

---

[17] However, you'd be amazed how many beautiful people are deeply insecure about their physical appearance, so Angelina could be triggered by such comments.

Therefore Ruiz says:

> "It is not important to me what you think about me, and I don't take it personally...it does not affect me because I know what I am. I don't have the need to be accepted...Others are going to have their own opinion according to their belief system, so nothing they think about me is really about me, it's about them...Whatever people do, feel, think or say, don't take it personally."

When you combine the insights that our core stories of deficiency are just meaningless thoughts with the commitment to not take anything personally, the fear of being hurt or rejected evaporates and your heart opens to giving and receiving love. This is true freedom. You can approach, or be approached, fearlessly. Nothing is at stake. You can lower your shields and tear down your walls. No matter how a relationship turns out, it doesn't mean you're unlovable or not good enough. It's not a reflection of who you are or what your future holds. If a partner cheats on you, or leaves you, or doesn't call you back, or doesn't ask you out, all of that is unpleasant, but it's about them, their opinions and what they want and believe. There's no threat in any of it. Nothing's at stake. The fear that those things could happen no longer has the power to keep you from opening your heart to a relationship. Your foot comes off the brake. You are free to do what you've been born to do, which is to love and be loved.

Attraction Factors

1. I shared a number of bullet point wonder questions on how the fear of being hurt and rejected can manifest in our lives. What's your strategy for protecting yourself from hurt and rejection?

— 10 —

The Fear of Engulfment

"There are two basic motivating forces: fear and love. When we are afraid, we pull back from life. When we are in love, we open to all that life has to offer with passion, excitement, and acceptance."

~ John Lennon

The fear of being rejected is the first reason we put our foot on the brake and keep ourselves out of a relationship. It's just too scary to let someone get close. But there's another equally prevalent and powerful fear that will keep us single and that is the fear of engulfment. This is the fear of losing your independence and freedom, or of being smothered and suffocated in some way. And if you're afraid of that, you're certainly not alone.

In the past, this fear was more of a male issue than a female one. Traditionally, it's been men who are commitment phobic and afraid of being controlled and smothered by relationships. My guess is men came up with phrases like, "getting hitched," "tying the knot," "the institution of marriage," and "the old ball and chain." But these days, women fear engulfment too.

Having grown up in environments where they saw their mothers, or other women, disappear and lose themselves, many women unconsciously believe that in order to have companionship, intimacy and family, they have to give up autonomy and control of their lives in order to get it.

The "Either/Or" Mentality

Whenever I coach someone—man or woman—who has the fear of engulfment keeping them single, they invariably see relationships in an "either/or" way. In other words, they believe that there are only two possible scenarios when it comes to intimacy: *EITHER* they can stay single and freely live their lives exactly as they see fit—*OR*—they can get in a relationship and give up their freedom and independence. You can't have both. It's either/or, not both/and. *You can't have your cake and eat it too*, or so it's thought.

The "Either/Or" mentality says you can't be in an amazing, intimate relationship AND be able to do whatever you want, whenever you want to do it. After all, compromise is the hallmark of a great relationship, isn't it? You can't be selfish. You have to be willing to make concessions, and maybe even negotiate a little or give up a few things in order to be in a relationship.

This is an incredibly common belief, and yet it's incredibly *uncommon* for someone to know just how profoundly this issue is controlling their relationship status. If you believe that a relationship means you must forfeit freedom, control and autonomy, you will sabotage your love life somewhere along the way.

Self-Sabotage

Here's an interesting insight, one that may help you get even more clarity as to which fear (rejection or engulfment) is keeping you single. If you fear rejection, you'll have issues at the very beginning of a relationship. Meaning, you'll have trouble mustering the courage to ask someone out (as I did), or you'll give off an energy that says, "stay away," and no one will approach you. So, for example, if you haven't had a date or a relationship in a long time, or if no one approaches you and asks you out, chances are very, very high that the fear of rejection is unconsciously operating in your life.

However, if the fear of engulfment is your issue, you'll have no problem getting into a relationship. It's when things begin to feel really good, when the relationship looks like it has the potential of going somewhere— that's when you'll sabotage things. You'll start finding faults, picking fights, or, and this is a really sneaky manifestation of the fear of engulfment, you'll find yourself interested in someone else and falsely interpret that attraction to mean something is lacking in your current relationship. But nothing is lacking. You're just scared. And if the fear gets too intense, you might even cheat on your partner! That's the ultimate way to sabotage a relationship and protect your independence.

No matter how the sabotage manifests, the closer you get to someone, the more your fear of being engulfed will intensify and you'll do something to get yourself out of the relationship. So, if you notice a pattern where your relationships start well, but then fizzle out or blow up in a month or two, the chances are very, very high that the fear of engulfment is behind it.

Sacred Selfishness

In summary then, many of us believe a relationship means being willing to give up your freedom and independence. It's not like *Burger King* where you can have it your way. You can't be both independent AND intimate. They are mutually exclusive, incompatible and irreconcilable.

This is, of course, a load of crap. It's just a story, an unexamined assumption. However, let's be clear about something. When you're in a committed relationship you do take your partner into consideration in all matters, because what you do with your time and money, and how you live your life does affect them. But that's a far cry from being controlled and/or smothered. I'm here to tell you that you don't have to give up anything in order to be in a great relationship. Zip, zero, zilch, nada. In fact:

One of the signs you're in a great relationship is the very fact that neither person is giving up anything of significance in order to be in the relationship.

Now, you may argue, "Baloney, Roy. Don't you have to give up having sex with other people to be in a relationship?" No, you don't. I sure don't. I have not given up sex with other women in order to be with my wife. My sex life is not being limited, constrained or controlled by my wife in any way. I'm in total control of my sex life and I have absolute freedom to do whatever I want. I am, however, choosing monogamy, not because she wants it, but because I want monogamy. It's my choice. No one is forcing it on me.

Furthermore, I have not given up a single thing in order to be with my wife. I go where I want, I spend money the way I want, I live the way I want, I make my schedule the way I want, I hang out with who I want, etc., etc.

Everything has been my choice. Monogamy is my choice. I have agreed to live within a budget, but it's been my choice too. I cross check my schedule with my wife's, but I do so because I choose to be considerate of her needs and plans. I discuss with her where I'm going and who I'm hanging out with, but I don't ask for permission. I live my life the way I want to, and so does she. Our independence is not limited in the least. In fact, both of us fight to protect each other's independence. If I ever found out that my wife was limiting herself because of our relationship, there'd be hell to pay. I demand that she fully follow her heart and live her life exactly the way she wants to live it. Nothing short of that would be tolerated. And that's goes both ways. We don't make concessions to be with one another, we don't negotiate or barter and we certainly don't compromise. *That's a 4-letter word in a conscious relationship.* If you need to compromise, you either

68

haven't been curious enough to discover a win/win solution or you don't belong together. I'm living exactly as I want to live—and so is she. We are sacredly selfish. Neither of us is giving up anything to be with the other. We have authentic intimacy AND absolute independence.

Releasing the Fear of Engulfment

How do you break this insane, self-sabotaging fear that a relationship is a hassle at best and a trap at worst? By asking one, simple question: *Is it true?* Is your "either/or" story, that you cannot be both independent AND intimate, true?

Remember, if something is true, then by definition, it's true for everyone. That means that no one has been able to figure out how to be intensely intimate with another human being and not lose themselves in the process. Is that true? Obviously not.

What is probably true, however, is that you have never seen it! I get that. Maybe you've lost yourself in previous relationships and you're afraid you'll fall into the same pattern. Perhaps your parents modeled co-dependence and engulfment. Maybe your friends do too. Perhaps you've never seen or experienced a healthy relationship that has both closeness and separateness. But that doesn't mean it's not possible. You can question your story. You can choose to believe that:

The opposite of your "either/or" story is just as true, or truer, than your story.

If you've never experienced or seen a relationship where two people were able to be fully close and yet fiercely independent, it makes sense that you'd have the "either/or" story. But you must recognize it's just your story and you must be willing to drop it or you'll never allow yourself to fully open up to love and intimacy. In other words, your relationship status will never change if you allow your story to go unexamined.

Space & Money

So let's examine two significant issues where the fear (story) of engulfment comes up: living space and money.

In terms of living space, some people don't like to sleep with someone in the same bed or in the same room or even live in the same house! Most people who are really private about their space keep themselves single because they think they have to give up their privacy in order to be in a relationship.

Is that true, though? Who says you have to sleep in the same bed, or even in the same house, for that matter? Who says you can't have one room for sex and two separate bedrooms for sleeping, reading or watching *your* favorite TV shows? And who says you can't live separately in a duplex or even next door to each other?

I once had a client who knew she never wanted to live with a guy. She didn't want to share her space, and all that goes with it. Consequently, she sabotaged all her relationships when they reached the point of marriage or cohabitation. I blew her mind when I said, "Why not buy houses right next to each other? You can have dinner together, have sex, watch TV, even sleep over whenever you want. You can do everything every other couple does, but he has his place and you have yours."

Our stories keep us from imagining how we can have our cake and eat it too. We must be unwilling to compromise and live in wonder and curiosity. You can have your living space just the way you want it AND be married or in a committed relationship.

Money is another area of life that people have huge, unexamined stories about. Who says you have to share your money? Can't you have separate bank accounts and divide up the expenses proportionally according to your individual incomes? Can't you make your own money and have complete control over how you spend, save or invest it? Can't you come up with some mutually agreed upon financial goals and then do whatever the hell you want with your money? Who says you have to be traditional and combine your income and accounts? Can't you create a financial arrangement that works for you both, no matter how counter-cultural it may be?

Furthermore, can't you go to different churches, have different friends, different hobbies and interests? Who says you have to adopt or be swallowed up by the other person's life and make it your own? Who says you have to have a bunch of things in common, anyway? Who makes up these rules and assumptions that keep us imprisoned and single? Is any of it true?

The fear of engulfment is similar to when people believed the earth was flat. If you explore your stories, you'll see that the fear of engulfment is just as much of an illusion as the earth is flat.

Brake Torque!

Do you know what brake torqueing is? It's when you rev up a car's engine while you have your foot on the brake. And just when the engine is roaring, you suddenly release the brake and the car peels out and takes off.

Well, although we have 4 more barriers to talk about, if you choose to release your fear of rejection and/or your stories about engulfment, your love life will "peel out" too. As I said earlier, releasing the Commitment Barrier may be the only thing necessary to attract lasting love.

Attraction Factors

1. Write out your story of how a relationship would limit your freedom or control you in some way. Describe how it would happen in your life.

2. Are you willing to see that the opposite of your story could be just as true or truer than your original story?

3. Write the opposite of your story. How do you feel about this possibility?

BARRIER FOUR

COMPLETION
Making Space for Love to Appear

"If you are incomplete with a former lover...then you are self-sabotaging your ability to create future relationship bliss...you cannot move forward if you are chained to the past."

~ Roy Biancalana

If you were going to give the inside of your home a complete makeover—new carpet, furniture, pictures, window coverings and such, one of the first things you'd do is get rid of the old stuff so that there's space for all your new, beautiful things. Likewise, as we seek to invite a new, beautiful person into our lives, we must make sure there's room in our hearts for them. All the emotional clutter has to go so that they can take up residence in our lives.

This fourth barrier to attracting lasting love is going to be your least favorite of all, because I'm going to ask you to face your past and do whatever is necessary to be complete with your former lovers, for as I said in my first book, "you cannot move forward if you are chained to the past."[18]

Here's how this section breaks down:

Chapter 11:   The Importance of a Clean Emotional Slate
Chapter 12:   The ABC's of Being Incomplete
Chapter 13:   How to Be Complete with Former Lovers
Chapter 14:   Completion Conversations

---

[18] Is it cheesy to quote yourself in your own book? :)

The Importance of a Clean Emotional Slate

"As I walked out the door toward my freedom, I knew that if I did not leave all the anger, hatred and bitterness behind that I would still be in prison."

~ Nelson Mandela

If you were to talk to most sports psychologists and ask them to name the single greatest mental skill an athlete needs in order to perform at his or her best, nearly all of them would say it's the ability to approach the next shot, pitch, at-bat, play, or point with *a clean emotional slate*. In other words, you have to approach the present moment without the slightest hint of negativity about, or attachment to, the past.

As important as it is in athletics, it is exponentially more important in your love life. If you are incomplete with former lovers, then you are sabotaging your ability to attract lasting love.

My goal in this chapter is twofold: First, I want to define what relationship incompletion means, but secondly and more importantly, I want to convince you to take this issue seriously. There's going to be a strong temptation to dismiss this barrier because it's such an unpleasant topic, and that would be tragic. So I'm going to share a few stories in the following chapters of how addressing this barrier revolutionized both my clients' lives and my life too. My hope is that they will inspire you to fully engage with this barrier and not blow it off. Our first step, though, is to define exactly what I mean by incompletion.

Defining Incompletion

Being incomplete with a former lover means to have an *ongoing positive or negative relationship with an ex, whether you personally interact with them regularly or not.* In other words, and to say it more playfully, if you still want to *kiss* or *kill* a former lover, you're incomplete. In either case, there's *a strong energetic charge towards them*, and consequently, you're still *involved* with them. You may or may not see or talk to them, but energetically, you're still involved with them. They are taking up heart-space, and therefore, there's no room for anyone else. It's like having a bunch of programs and applications open and running on your computer. The memory-space is "involved" and the machine will slow down. Likewise, incompletion slows down, or even "crashes," your love life.

Examine Your Heart

Most people recognize the importance of this issue *in other people's lives.* It's definitely a "red flag" or a deal-breaker to meet someone who appears to be seriously hung up on, or in ugly drama with their ex. However, when it's happening in their own life it's not taken that seriously. If I had a nickel for every time a client has told me that their positive or negative feelings about an ex don't matter, I'd be a rich man.

I am really concerned that you are one of those people, that you don't think *your* feelings toward your ex are that big of a deal. Please don't read this section of the book thinking this topic applies to others and not you. Look in the mirror. Examine your heart. I rarely meet someone who is fully complete with their past relationships. They don't see the cause and effect relationship between their inability to attract their ideal partner and their ongoing emotional, physical or logistical involvement with an ex. They don't make the connection—but there's probably a huge connection.

If there were ever a "Wizard of Oz" type issue, one that works behind the scenes, "turning the knobs and pulling the levers," this would be it. Incompletion sabotages our love lives in 4 dramatic, tragic, and often unconscious, ways.

4 Dangers of Being Incomplete

1. Projection will Reign. Being incomplete with former lovers means we're holding on to the past, keeping it alive. This causes us to project that past onto any new potential partner. We're not seeing them for who they truly are; we're seeing them through the lens of the past. For example, if previous partners have been untrustworthy, then you will approach a new relationship with guarded, prove-yourself-to-me, suspicion. This fear-based energy can be felt, especially by quality people, and they will be appropriately turned off. *The result is that you'll chase away the very people you most want to attract.*

2. Partners will Replicate. Whatever word or phrase you use—God, the Universe, Spirit, or Divine Intelligence—that Presence is committed to your evolution and growth. Every experience is either allowed to occur or divinely orchestrated to teach us an important lesson. If we don't learn the intended lessons, those experiences will repeat until we do. Every partner is an ally and a teacher, perfectly suited to help us learn the most important things for our growth.[19] If we haven't learned those lessons, we'll attract the same kinds of partners over and over again until we do.

3. Patterns will Repeat. If we attract the same kinds of partners again and again, then it stands to reason that we'll experience the same patterns and pain again and again too. Incompletion creates a vicious, repeating loop. This was beautifully illustrated by the movie *Groundhog Day*.[20] Bill Murray's character, Phil Connors, was not allowed to experience a new day until he made peace with the previous one.

4. Power will Reduce. The final dangerous result of being incomplete is that it reduces our attraction power. Take men, for example. What makes a man truly attractive? It's more than his appearance, sense of humor or financial status. It's deeper qualities like clarity, presence and openness.[21] But when a man is incomplete, his clarity is fuzzy, his presence is distracted and his heart is closed. He's not magnetic or attractive. For women, incompletion has a similar impact on their attraction power. Her true attractiveness is far deeper than conventional beauty. It's her playfulness, sensuality and vulnerability. In other words, it's her inner beauty or radiance.[22] But when she's still energetically involved with an ex, her "shine" is darkened and her radiance is reduced. She, too, is not magnetic or attractive.

So unless these 4 dangers sound like a good time to you, I suggest you take incompletion seriously. If you're willing to do that, the first order of business, then, is to determine whether or not, or to what extent, you are incomplete with any of your former lovers. That is the topic of the next chapter.

---

[19] "Allies" is one of the 7 commitments in my *Dating Manifesto*, found in Appendix I.

[20] Enjoy. http://bit.ly/1lZC4Ll

[21] We'll talk about this in Barrier 6.

[22] We'll talk about this in Barrier 6 too.

Attraction Factors

1. Make a list of your most significant intimate relationships.

2. Which ones are you still "involved" with, positively or negatively.

3. Of the 4 dangers of being incomplete, which one stands out to you the most and why?

— 12 —

The ABC's of Being Incomplete

"Nothing ever happened in the past that can prevent you from being present now; and if the past cannot prevent you from being present now, what power does it have?"

~ Eckhart Tolle

Is there space in your heart for love to appear? That is the central question we're focusing on in this section of the book. Is there room in your life for someone new, or are you still involved with someone from your past, be it emotionally, physically or logistically? If so, then there's a "No Vacancy" sign hanging on the door of your heart and you'll never attract a *healthy* relationship.

I've already spent a considerable amount of time encouraging you not to dodge, diminish or dismiss this issue, so I won't repeat myself. The purpose of this chapter is to determine if, or to what extent, you are incomplete with any of your former relationships. Simply put, you are incomplete if you are *involved* (1) Emotionally, (2) Physically, or (3) Logistically, or any combination of the three. Let's look at each of those categories one at a time.

1. Emotional Incompletion

This is, by far, the most common way we are incomplete with former lovers, and therefore, it demands the most attention. So, let's break it down by making it as easy as learning your ABC's. Being emotionally incomplete manifests itself as **A**ttachment, **B**itterness or being **C**losed.

A—Attachment

If you're still hung up on, in love with, missing, wanting or grieving a former lover, you are emotionally attached, and therefore incomplete. There's no room in your heart for someone new. It doesn't matter whether you have actual contact with them or not. They may have passed away. But if you're still emotionally involved with them, your heart-space is occupied. This isn't wrong or bad. It's just something to be faced.

When my fiancée broke off our engagement, I was crushed. On the deepest level, I knew it was for the best, but I was still devastated. I missed her. I loved her. I wanted her back. I thought about her all the time and talked about her to anyone who'd listen—even other women I dated! Though we didn't see or talk to one another, I was still *involved* with her.

If any of the following bullet points are true for you, you're still emotionally attached to a former lover.

- Your ex is a central topic of conversation with friends, family, a coach, God or even people you date
- You miss them and want them back
- You still cry sometimes when you think of them and your relationship
- You rehash and relive your relationship in your mind
- You masturbate or fantasize about them
- You follow (stalk?) them on social media or drive past their work or home
- They're the last thought of the day and the first thought in the morning
- You have a bunch of pictures of them (one is still in your wallet or purse)
- There's a shrine of sorts in your home concerning them

Ruthless honesty time: Are you emotionally attached to a former lover? If so, it's not bad or wrong, it just means your heart-space is cluttered and you have to do some completion work, which is discussed in the next chapter.

B—Bitterness

A second manifestation of being emotionally incomplete is the opposite of being attached. It's feeling bitter and angry towards a former lover. Hostility, hate, resentment, blame, holding a grudge, bad-mouthing them to your kids, taking them to court out of spite, seeking financial punishment or revenge, and even gossiping about them are sure signs that you're still *involved* with them. In other words, when there's drama between the two of you, or merely within your own heart, you're incomplete. Either situation leaves no emotional space in your heart for someone new.

As I said earlier, this is easy to spot in others. We've all been on dates where the other person drones on and on about what a bitch or bastard their ex was. Sure, they're not in love with them; in fact, they hate their guts. But either way, they're not free of them. Both are equally dangerous signs of incompletion. They're still *involved*. The issue is, of course, do we recognize this in our own lives and are we taking it seriously or are we dismissing it?

Here's a completion principle:

> **When you're truly complete with a former lover,
> you feel mostly indifferent and neutral towards them,
> wanting neither to kiss nor kill them.**

Ruthless honesty time again: Do you feel bitter and angry towards a former lover? Is there a lot of drama between the two of you, or merely within your own heart? Again, don't beat yourself up if there is. Just recognize that you've got to let go of the negativity so that there's space in your heart for someone new.

C—Closed

The third way we can be emotionally incomplete is when we allow past pain to fester and ferment in us until it shuts us down and closes our hearts. Deception, divorce or the death of a loved one can bring intense feelings of betrayal and grief. These feelings can calcify in our hearts to the point where we become cold, cynical, callous and closed toward love and relationships. In other words, we create walls around our hearts.

One of my female clients used to complain that when she was out with her girlfriends, guys approached them, but never her. While she was an attractive, successful woman, I wasn't surprised, because I felt her closure in our sessions. She never faced me and rarely made eye contact. When she did look at me, she had to turn her head pretty far to do so. She also kept her arms crossed most of the time. If she was giving me the "stay away" signal, I could only imagine the message she gave off in public.[23] This woman was terrified of letting men get close.

Here are some practical manifestations of a closed, walled off heart:

- Crossed arms, chin down, body turned away, excessive space between you and others
- Lack of smiling, little or no eye contact, rarely touching others

---

[23] Herein lies a real benefit of working with an opposite sex coach. While there are clear boundaries in a coach/client relationship, I am a man and she is a woman. I'm certain that had this client been working with a woman, her body language would have been dramatically different. But working with me allowed her unconscious closure toward men to surface and we could work on it.

- Burying your face in your phone or dressing ultra-conservatively
- Rarely initiating conversation or excessively talking (both keep people away)
- People say you're shy, or hard to read, or they don't know what you're feeling or that you're difficult to get to know or that you're "mysterious" (this is not a compliment)
- Having trust issues, a long list of desired qualities in a life partner, or being excessively picky
- "Never again" statements like, "I'll never let *that* happen to me" or "I will *not* let a man hurt me like that again" or "That's the *last* time I get that vulnerable and open up"
- Sweeping generalizations like, "All men are players and want only one thing." "All women are either needy and want you to take care of them, especially financially, or they're angry, ball-busters"

These are all subtle (or not so subtle) manifestations of a closed heart. Being incomplete with a former lover means you are still *involved* with them emotionally by being attached, bitter or closed.

2. Physical Incompletion

The second way you can be incomplete, and therefore sabotage your ability to attract lasting love, is if you're physically still involved with a former lover. At first glance, it seems obvious that if you're still hooking up with your ex, you're still involved, but many people don't see it that way. I have a number of clients who believe that as long as they're not dating anyone, they don't see a problem with hooking up with their ex every so often or even having a "friends with benefits" relationship. Their perspective is, "If I'm not cheating on anyone, what's the harm? I'll stop seeing them as soon as I meet someone."

Now, I have no moral issue with hooking up with an ex or having casual sex. None whatsoever. I don't think it's ultimately satisfying, but I have no moral qualms about it. However, if you agree with the perspective that there's no harm in hooking up with an ex as long as you're not dating anyone, you've completely missed the point of this entire section. What I'm saying is that you can no more attract a *healthy* relationship into your life while you're having "meaningless sex" with an ex, any more than you can pour water into a glass that's already full. There's no room. (I also seriously doubt that it's "just sex," and that there's no emotional connection between you.)

The day I met my wife at that conference, if she somehow found out that I had hooked up with my ex fiancée the night before, would she have felt there was space in my heart for her? Obviously not. I'm not saying you're supposed to share your sexual history with someone on a first date, but if that had happened, I definitely would not have wanted her to find out about it, and what does that say?

I'll take it one step further. Even if there's no sexual relationship, if you are having personal and intimate conversations, connecting with an ex in a way that goes way beyond financial or childcare issues, you're still involved. There may be some special circumstances that we could discuss, but basically, if you're communicating or consummating with a former lover, you're still involved with them and there is no room in your heart for a new relationship.

3. Logistical Incompletion

Lastly, if logistical matters concerning finances, property, animals, children, visitation and such are not fully settled and separated by clear boundaries, you're incomplete and still involved. Having ongoing drama and confusion concerning such matters saps your energy and clutters your heart-space.

I have a friend who has not lived with his ex for years, but they're still not officially divorced because he wants to stay on her insurance. Now, this isn't bad or wrong, but would any woman in her right mind seriously date a man in that situation? Logistically, he's still involved.

A similar situation happens when a divorced couple's house is "under water." They don't want to take a huge financial hit by selling it, so they continue living together, albeit in separate bedrooms. Again, this isn't bad or wrong it's just a situation that a wise person would stay away from because the relationship is ongoing and logistically incomplete.

Finally, to be impeccable in this area, I encourage my clients to evaluate every item that they own and determine if there is any energetic charge in regards to things like pictures, clothing, jewelry, beds, cars or even houses. If any item keeps the past alive by triggering sadness or attachment, it might need to be discarded.

For example, my ex fiancée bought me a pair of jeans. She said they made me look really good. I had to get rid of them because they reminded me of her and made me feel sad. But she also bought me a watch that I have to this day. It doesn't trigger anything in me. It's just a watch.

There are no rules on this sort of thing. What triggers you might be different from what triggers me or anyone else. The important thing is to cut the cords to your past, whether they're emotional, physical or logistical and make space for love to appear.

Attraction Factors

1. Is there a former lover with whom you're incomplete because you're still attached, bitter or closed? If so, what are you going to do about it this week?

2. What would it mean to cut the physical or psychological cords between you and a former lover? What would have to stop immediately?

3. What logistical issues are unsettled and incomplete with a former lover and what are you going to do about it this week?

— 13 —

How To Be Complete With Former Lovers

"Being complete means to have expressed all my feelings, saying everything (including any withholds, as well as appreciations), and then taking full, healthy responsibility by acknowledging and owning how I participated in all the ways the relationship went.

~ Grace Caitlin

There are three critical steps to being complete with a former lover. They are *very* challenging, to put it mildly. In fact, if there were ever a topic that might require a private coaching session (or two or three), this would be it. If you get tripped up here, please reach out to me for support.[24]

I also want you to know that I've climbed the three steps you're about to take and done everything I'm going to ask you to do. And honestly, I hated every single step. The truth may set you free, but in my experience, it sure pisses you off at first. But if it weren't for these three steps, I would not be with the woman I am today. These steps cleared all the clutter out of my heart and made space for love to appear.

The three steps to being complete with former lovers are, (1) Take Healthy Responsibility, (2) Give Healthy Forgiveness, and (3) Have a Healthy Completion Conversation. We'll deal with the first two in this chapter and the third in the next chapter.

Step 1: Take Healthy Responsibility

Karen came to work with me because she and her ex husband were in so much drama that it was scaring away the men she dated. They shared joint custody of their son and whenever they interacted with one another, it got really ugly and nasty. The other men saw the ongoing drama and didn't want any part of it. Frankly, she couldn't blame them, and that's why she came to me for help.

The drama between Karen and her ex-husband stemmed from his long-held belief that, even though they had been married for over 10 years, she

---

[24] roy@coachingwithroy.com

had never gotten over her ex-boyfriend and still loved him. In his mind, their marriage failed because her heart was never truly his. For years she denied this, and instead, blamed the demise of their marriage on his anger issues.

After a number of sessions with Karen, I finally said, "Do you think your ex could be right? Do you still love your ex-boyfriend? Is it possible that your heart was never truly his?" There was a long silence on the phone, then, "yes."

I admired her honesty and then I said, "Karen, if you want to end the drama between you and your ex-husband, and not have this issue chase away another good man, then you have to go to him, and tell him to his face that he was right. You have to own up to the fact that your feelings for your ex-boyfriend sabotaged your relationship, and that the two of you really never had a chance because of it."

More silence. I could tell the ego was kicking in. "What about his anger issues? Our problems weren't all *my* fault!"

"Granted," I said. "Perhaps he does have anger issues. But how much of his anger came from feeling you were still in love with someone else and wouldn't admit it?"

She courageously said, "Probably a lot of it."

"Yes, tell him that too. Tell him that you understand how your feelings for your ex-boyfriend made him crazy with jealousy and anger."

The ego still fought, though.

"He's going to say 'I told you so!' I can't stand the thought of him being right and rubbing my face in it!"

"Karen, do you want to be right, or do you want peace and the possibility of a new, intimate relationship? Of course it's not *all* your fault. Your relationship was co-created. *But you have to be willing to own the fact that without your part, the relationship would never have gone as it did."*

To her credit, Karen decided to have that completion conversation with her ex. And at first, he did spew his anger at her, but he eventually calmed down and their relationship shifted dramatically. In fact, she later told me it was like a miracle. They aren't chummy, of course, but there's no bitterness and drama between them anymore.

Then, we set about the task of releasing her lingering attachment to her ex-boyfriend. She didn't want to sabotage another relationship the same way. We also discovered some unconscious emotional walls she had built in response to her controlling, domineering father, and when we tore them down, she was finally able attract a great guy and sustain a healthy relationship.

The first step to being complete with a former lover, then, is to take healthy responsibility for any attachment, bitterness or closure that exists within you. It's putting into practice everything we learned from the Change Barrier in part 2 of this book. When you choose the creator mindset over the victim mindset, you'll be given insight that will allow you to dissolve anything that's cluttering your heart and making it impossible for a new person to take up residence in you.

Step 2: Give Healthy Forgiveness

The second step to being complete with former lovers is by giving healthy forgiveness. Most people really struggle with this, however. They know that they should forgive someone, but how do you do that when they really hurt or betrayed you?

Once we see what our responsibility was for how a particular relationship went, without discounting or excusing anyone else's behavior, the blame and bitterness drops away and a deeper understanding arises. You see how your relationship's dynamic was *co-created*. This doesn't mean you should get back together with your ex, it just means there's a realization that both of you were playing out your unconscious patterns and personas, and mixed together, they created the "stew" that was your relationship.

If you are committed to playing the victim then you will always struggle with forgiveness. But choosing to see yourself as the creator, that life is not happening "to you," but "by you," then the whole issue of forgiveness gets turned on its ear, doesn't it? In fact, the only one to forgive is yourself, for not being aware of how you've created your life the way you have.

Do you see that? Forgiveness, as it's normally taught, comes from a victim mindset. THEY are the villain. THEY did something horrible "to you." But if you don't view life in a victim/villain way, then there is no need to forgive anyone other than yourself.

Bottom line: If you feel the need to forgive someone, you're playing the victim. If you need someone else's forgiveness, you're playing the villain. Forgiveness does not exist in conscious relationships. Only self-forgiveness does.

The Puppy Metaphor

I have found, however, that even when people understand this, they still struggle with making sense of the horrible and hurtful things people do and say. A conscious approach to forgiveness isn't about putting your head in the sand and singing *kumbaya*. People do shitty things. There's no denying this. This is where the "Puppy Metaphor" comes in handy.

What does a puppy do when you bring it home from the kennel or purchase it from a litter? The little thing pees on your carpet and chews on your shoes, right? That's annoying, of course, but is the puppy being bad? Is it doing something wrong? No, of course not. That's what puppies do—they pee on the carpet and chew on shoes. You will train the puppy, but for now, you could say that the puppy is acting and behaving according to its level of maturity, isn't it? It's reflecting its level of consciousness or understanding.

Here's the punch line: Every human being, in every moment (and that includes you and me), is just like that puppy. We are always acting and behaving according to our level of maturity or state of consciousness. We are, in a sense, "peeing on the carpet and chewing on shoes." We're doing the only thing we know how to do. We are reflecting our stage of development—always—and we can *never* do otherwise.

The puppy cannot act beyond its level of maturity. That would be impossible. A baby can't do ballet. It can only crawl, if that. We can only act, behave and choose in accordance with our level of understanding and maturity. You cannot say someone should know better any more than you could say the puppy should know better. Every single person, from *Osama bin Laden* to *Pope Francis,* is acting and behaving according to their level of consciousness in the moment. It cannot be otherwise.

Here's the insight that will set you free from regret, bitterness toward others or self-hatred:

> **It's not that we are doing the best that we can,**
> **it's that we are doing the only thing we can.**

This is why spiritual teachers have always said there are no mistakes and that there's no such thing as "evil." There are only "puppies," peeing and chewing, reflecting their level of understanding.

Jesus understood this. When he was being crucified (which, by the way, is way worse than anything you or I have been through), he prayed, *"Father, forgive them for they do not know what they're doing."*[25]

He's saying, "Father, they're puppies, peeing on the carpet, chewing on shoes. They're doing the only thing they know how to do. Forgive them.

---

[25] Luke 23:34

They're doing what they think is right, and given their state of understanding, they are!"

Now, this does not mean we should let people continue to do and say harmful things to us. People like Osama bin Laden should be stopped and we should hold people accountable for their actions and set firm boundaries. But the bitterness and anger we have towards others, or towards ourselves, drops away once we see that everyone is doing the only thing that they can.

The first two steps in being complete with past relationships is to take healthy responsibility for your part in how the relationship went, and to give healthy forgiveness by realizing that both of you were "puppies," peeing on the carpet and chewing on shoes. The third and final step, *Completion Conversations*, is covered in the next chapter.

Attraction Factors
1. For each of your incomplete relationships, describe what your part was in how the relationship went. (If this is still fuzzy, you'll learn more about this in the next section of the book.)

2. How do you feel about the "puppy metaphor?" Describe your insights and how it changes your perspective.

Completion Conversations

"Therefore, confess your sins to one another...so that you may be healed."

~ James 5:16

I grew up in Chicago. It's an incredible city, but the winters are brutal. The harsh weather seems to last forever, which is why March was my least favorite month of the year. By then, I'd had enough. I was ready for it to warm up. But, unfortunately, the weather in March is still very unpleasant.

I imagine that you feel like that right about now. The Completion Barrier is like a long, harsh Chicago winter. It's no fun and I'm sure you're ready for some nicer "weather." It's coming, I promise. Barriers 5-7 are much more enjoyable and pleasant. But this chapter is "March"—one more month of nasty weather before things get better.

Confession is Good for the Soul

When you get curious about your relationships and take healthy responsibility (step 1), you'll discover that you required your partners and your relationships to be exactly as they were. Seeing this, a new spaciousness will open in your heart. You won't need to forgive anyone for anything because no one did anything "to you." As Jimmy Buffett sang, *"Some people claim that there's a woman (or man) to blame, but I know, it's my own damn fault."* That is why we've said the only forgiveness needed is self-forgiveness (step 2). When these first two steps are taken, attachments will release, bitterness will dissolve and closure will relax.

But in order to be *fully* complete, there's one final step. Like Karen in the last chapter, you have to tell your former lover(s) what you discovered about yourself and how you contributed to your relationship's demise. Something magical happens when we speak our truth, reveal our secrets, share our appreciations and confess our "sins." It releases us from the prison of the past and opens our hearts to the future. Admittedly, this can be a real punch in your ego's gut, but if you really want to open up space in your heart for love to appear, a very short completion conversation is essential.

In this chapter, I want to explain how to have this conversation and then share the story of how being complete changed my love life. It will illustrate how powerful completing is and hopefully it will inspire you to have your own completion conversations.

Step 3: Completion Conversations

To understand how to have a completion conversation, let's discuss Who, What, When, Where and How. (Why was answered in the last three chapters.)

Who do you have a completion conversation with?

The only people you need to have a completion conversation with are those with whom you feel a strong positive or negative charge towards. I dated many women, but there were only three that met that criteria: my ex wife, my ex fiancée and a woman I dated for about 4 months.

What do you say in this conversation?

The topic of conversation is limited to four things: (1) Share what you've learned about yourself. Tell them what you're taking responsibility for. Do not share your opinions about them and what they should take responsibility for. That will just create more drama. This is a one-way conversation. If they say something, you can listen, but you're not requiring anything from them, nor are you looking for any response from them. This is simply about you being honest and complete with them. (2) Reveal any secrets you've kept from them. Everything must come out. Everything. (3) Express what you appreciate about them and your relationship. Be specific. (4) If there are logistical matters to clear up, address them and also clarify any boundaries concerning future contact and communication.

When should you have this conversation?

If you want to open up space in your heart and attract lasting love, have this conversation as soon as possible. But you should only have this conversation *after* talking with a wise, trusted friend or coach first. Get someone's feedback and ask them if they feel you're ready to do this. Many people try to have these talks while they're still playing the victim. If you do, it will blow up in your face. This is the *last* step in the process for a reason, and it often takes some time to get to the point where you're ready to have this talk. My final completion conversation with my ex fiancée happened about 14 months after our break up. I was not ready to do it before then. I was still attached and bitter. If any of that remains, it means you haven't completed steps one and two.

Where do you have this conversation?

In-person and face-to-face is preferable, but there are a number of caveats here. If there is a huge distance between you, or if you feel it would get ugly, or if you feel they could be violent or verbally abusive, you can and should use the phone or send an email. If you can't locate them or if they've passed away, you can role-play with a friend or coach.

How does this conversation work?

The entire conversation should take no longer than 5 minutes. One of the principles of conscious communication is that important things should be communicated in one outbreath. Long discussions will lead to story-telling and drama. Sit down, share your insights, secrets, appreciations and boundaries, listen to any response they have, and then walk away. Your conversation will included phrases like: "I want you to know that I take full responsibility for..." or "I never told you that..." or "I appreciate you for..." and "I'd like our future contact to be limited to..."

A Completion Story[26]

When I met MaryMargaret, we had some twists and turns in the first couple of months of our relationship. We weren't connecting somehow. We were physically attracted to one another, we enjoyed each other's company and we were spiritually compatible, but for some reason she just didn't seem emotionally responsive to me. She seemed a bit shut down and distant. After a number of dates, our relationship fizzled in an awkward and confusing way. Like a car running out of gas, we just drifted to a stop. It was very strange.

A week or so after that, I was having a phone session with my coach, Diana, and we realized that I still had some unfinished business with my ex fiancée, Julie.[27] Though it had been 14 months since we had broken up, I still had some negative energy toward her. Diana said I needed to call her and get complete with this. And I did.

---

[26] This story originally appeared in chapter 21 of my first book, *Relationship Addiction—A Memoir.*

[27] "Julie" is not her real name. In fact, all the names in this book have been changed except for my coach's and my wife's.

My discussion with Julie got kind of heated initially because I played the victim and blamed her for what she did to me. But then I came to my senses, took responsibility and shared my truth with her in accordance with the principles above. The conversation ended beautifully with us sharing kind words of gratitude and appreciation for one another. It was actually a sweet moment between us. It felt like a tender exhale. We were complete.

A few days after that, I found myself thinking of MaryMargaret. I felt as if we were incomplete as well, and because it went so well with Julie, I decided to call her too. I shared with MaryMargaret that I wasn't comfortable with how our relationship had drifted to a stop and that I wanted to meet and get some closure. I had no thought of her and me being a couple again. None whatsoever. Nor did she. In fact, I later learned that she reluctantly agreed to meet me at all.

When we got together, she was just as I remembered her: sweet, spiritual, beautiful, and of course, distant. But then, not 10 minutes into our conversation, something strange started happening. Her energy and demeanor began to change, right before my eyes. Previously, she was walled-off and closed. Now she was opening up and coming to life, mysteriously morphing into this playful, warm, sensual, flirtatious and outright energetic woman. She lit up the room. I was dumbfounded.

It was so obvious, I said, "What the hell is happening to you?" She knew what I was talking about and seemed as confused by her shifting energy as I was. I told her that I had no idea what was going on but that I was having second thoughts about "us" and was thinking maybe we ought to consider dating again. She beamed. We both did. As we walked toward the restaurant door, this formerly distant woman grabbed my ass—right in public! We ended up making out in her car like a couple of teenagers!

We have since talked about that night many, many times. It brings a smile to both of our faces. But it never made sense to me until I connected my completion conversation with Julie to MaryMargaret's "Jekyll and Hyde" transformation. There was a cause and effect relationship! She had no cognitive awareness that I was still energetically stuck in the past and incomplete with Julie back when we first met, but her body could *feel* it.

Within ten minutes of sitting and talking with me, again without knowing I had completed with Julie, her body could *feel* that I was now fully present, and she opened up like a flower. *My incomplete relationship with Julie had shut down MaryMargaret's heart!* And when I completed with Julie, her body told her that it was now okay to let go and take up residence in my heart, for finally there was room.

The lesson is this: Not only does being complete with former lovers open space in your heart for something new, it can even open up space in someone else's heart as well. If I had not swallowed my pride and called my ex fiancée to complete our relationship, then the amazing woman I met at that personal growth workshop in Chicago would have been just a memory, and never my wife.

I hope this story inspires you to find the courage to take healthy responsibility, give healthy forgiveness and have a healthy completion conversation. It was the best thing I ever did.

Her

I want to close this section of the book by sharing with you a great example of a completion letter. It comes from the 2013 movie, *Her*[28], starring, *Joaquin Phoenix*. He's playing a guy named "Theodore," who is letting go of his attachment to his former lover, "Catherine." If you look closely, you'll see all three steps beautifully expressed.

> Dear Catherine,
> I've been sitting here thinking about all the things I wanted to apologize to you for. All the pain we caused each other, everything I put on you - everything I needed you to be or needed you to say. I'm sorry for that. I will always love you because we grew up together. And you helped make me who I am. I just wanted you to know there will be a piece of you in me always, and I'm grateful for that. Whatever someone you become, and wherever you are in the world, I'm sending you love. You're my friend till the end.
> > Love, Theodore."

Attraction Factors

1. With whom do you need to have a completion conversation?

2. When and how will you do it?

---

[28] Here it is in video form. Gives me chills to this day. http://bit.ly/10bHCsM

BARRIER FIVE

(de)CONSTRUCTION
Recognize and Release Your Relationship Persona

"Remember this: 100% of spiritual growth, development and unfoldment is about letting go of something; it's not about getting or acquiring something. It's about releasing something."

~ Michael Bernard Beckwith

Someone once asked *Michelangelo* how he was able to perfectly sculpt *David* from a huge piece of marble. His answer was profound. He said that *David* was always there, shrouded within the marble. His task was simply to chip away everything that didn't belong.

That is exactly our task in this section of the book. Think of me as "Michelangelo," wielding a spiritual chisel, and yourself as "David," this amazing person whose magnificent essence is shrouded by something called a *Relationship Persona*. This persona self is the fifth barrier that stands in the way of your ability to attract lasting love and we're going to "chip away" at it until the only thing that remains is your authentic self.

Here's how this section unfolds:

Chapter 15:   The Relationship Groundhog Day Syndrome
Chapter 16:   A Little Ditty About Roy and Julie
Chapter 17:   Shape-Shifting
Chapter 18:   Persona Parties

— 15 —

The Relationship Groundhog Day Syndrome

"Wherever you go, there you are."

~ Confucius

When you look at your relationship history, do you notice a tendency to attract a certain kind of person? Even if they had very different backgrounds and personalities, were they the same *type* of person? Meaning, were they needy, controlling, crazy, dishonest, passive, absent, victims, angry, addicted, unstable, unavailable, workaholic, wounded or something like that? In other words, *is there a certain type of person you seem to attract?*

Additionally, do you notice a particular pattern that your relationships take? Is there a theme or a dynamic that seems to repeat itself? For example, do you rarely get a second date? Do you end up in the "friend zone," or do you seem to rescue "damsels in distress" or "wounded soldiers"? Maybe your pattern is to have great chemistry, but little or no compatibility or vice versa. Perhaps you find yourself in confusing relationships that never seem to go anywhere, or that you put in all the effort and the other person is distant or noncommittal. Whatever it is, *do you notice a repeating dynamic or pattern?*

This phenomenon of attracting the same types of partners and/or patterns over and over again is something I playfully call, "The Relationship Groundhog Day Syndrome."[29] It is extremely common. In fact, I rarely meet someone who can't describe their own version of Relationship Groundhog Day.

Breaking Free

It would be incredibly tragic to have worked through all the barriers in this book and then turn around and repeat your relationship history—again. Just the thought of that should make your skin crawl. Unfortunately, unless we understand The Relationship Groundhog Day Syndrome and break free

---

[29] Here's the trailer. Notice the line at the very end: *"Life has a funny way of repeating itself."* Oh, how true. http://bit.ly/1lZC4Ll

of it, we will do *exactly* that. For no matter how determined we are to do otherwise, we will continue to attract the same kinds of partners, patterns, problems and pain—over and over again—until we break free.

Changing this dynamic begins as all change does, by shifting from Victim Consciousness to Creator Consciousness. Groundhog Day is not happening "to you," but "by you." You must claim responsibility for your experience and become curious as to what you're doing to invite the same people and patterns into your life.

Such curiosity would sound like, *"Hmmm, I wonder how I'm responsible for this pattern in my life? What am I doing to attract it, or even require it?"* It takes a brave person to ask such questions. Frankly, it took me a long time (and a lot of pain) before I was willing to ask them.

The victim mentality had a strong hold on me for a long time. For years, I assumed that my pattern of attracting "damsels in distress" was just really bad luck. It never occurred to me that I was unconsciously *seeking* women who were overwhelmed and needing to be taken care of. But when I asked those wonder questions, I discovered that a *Relationship Persona* was running my life and it actually *needed* that kind of woman.

Let me explain.

The Puzzle Metaphor

Most of us have put puzzles together at one time or another, so we know that every puzzle piece has a particular shape and the idea is to find the piece that matches it. We can't put any two random pieces together. They have to match. They have to fit together. This is the exact reason why we attract the same partners and the same patterns over and over again.

We are like pieces of a puzzle with a particular psychological and emotional "shape," which was formed by past experiences and early childhood conditioning. And just as an actual puzzle piece doesn't fit with any random piece, so our particular "shape" doesn't fit with just any random person's "shape" either. *We fit only with those whose "shape" matches ours.* In a sense, we are the "cookies" to their "milk," and vice versa. We go together.

Relationship Personas

This psycho-emotional "shape" is called a *relationship persona*. It is not the real you, but a "person" you become, or a role you play, in order to get the love and attention you desire. For example, my relationship persona, the role I played, has always been "Roy the Rescuer."[30] My past experiences and childhood conditioning taught me that if I wanted to be close to a woman, I had to take care of her every need.

Now, in order for "Roy the Rescuer" to operate, he has to have someone to rescue, doesn't he? Superman needs Lois Lane. My "shape" as "Roy the Rescuer" *REQUIRES* a woman with a complimentary, matching "shape," someone we could call, "Debbie the Damsel." The two are a perfect match! They go together like cookies and milk. Rescuers need victims and vice versa. In fact, they more than need each other; they *require* each other.

Furthermore, notice that as long as I remain "Roy the Rescuer," I'll *always* attract, "Debbie the Damsel." It cannot be otherwise. My "shape" demands it. Groundhog Day will never end because she's the only puzzle piece that fits my "shape."

This leads to what I hope will be an "aha" insight:

As long as your "shape" remains the same, you will always attract the same kinds of partners into your life.

Until we identify our particular "shape" and shift it, we will forever be stuck in Relationship Groundhog Day, repeating our relationship history over and over again.

Identifying Your Persona

Now, here's where it gets really crazy. *We don't know we're doing any of this!* We are completely unaware that we're in the grip of a relationship persona. They form so early in our lives that by the time we reach adulthood, we mistake the persona self for our authentic self. *We think the persona is who we really are.* Like a Broadway actor who plays a role for so long that he actually begins thinking he *IS* the role, so we've been playing our roles for so long that we actually think it's who we really are.

This was true of me. I used to think I was just a really nice, unselfish guy who loved to take care of his woman and spoil her. I actually called myself, "The World's Greatest Boyfriend."[31] I had no idea that I was actually terrified that a woman would never want me unless I devoted my life to

---

[30] His official name is "Casanova" and you'll hear more about him in the next chapter. For now, though, I'll call him "Roy the Rescuer" because it describes his behavior more clearly than does "Casanova."

[31] That is the actual title of Chapter 12 in my first book, *Relationship Addiction—A Memoir*

taking care of hers. "Roy the Rescuer" and all the wonderful things he did, were not authentic expressions of love they were manifestations of fear and insecurity. But I was completely unaware of those motivations. I thought I was being my authentic self.

So how do you identify your relationship persona when you're unaware that you even have one? Answer: By the "shape" it attracts. Remember, your "shape" always attracts its match. So simply look at the kinds of partners and patterns you're attracting and ask what persona or role you must be playing to attract it. For example, when I noticed my pattern was attracting overwhelmed women who needed to be taken care of, *that meant my persona had to be that of a rescuer or hero.* They match each other.

Here are a few examples of matching personas or roles. They go together like cookies and milk. Remember, you can be either and maybe even more than one. The point is that no matter what your persona is, it requires a matching playmate.

"Cookies"	**"Milk"**
• Rescuers	Damsels
• Players	Suckers
• Addicts	Enablers
• Control Freaks	Doormats
• Bad Boys	Church Girls
• Narcissists	Self-Forgetters
• Wounded Soldiers	Nurses
• Clingers	Runners
• Drama Queens (or Kings)	Firefighters

If you want to attract lasting love, you have to become conscious of your psycho-emotional "shape" and shift it. Otherwise you will relive your relationship history over and over again.

Finally, there are as many matching personas as there are patterns. If you don't see yours on my short list, come up with your own and name the complimentary persona it requires. *I consider the work I did to recognize and release, "Roy the Rescuer," to be the single greatest reason I was able to attract and sustain a healthy relationship.*

Know Thyself

"Know Thyself" were the words inscribed above the entrance to the temple of Apollo at Delphi, site of the sacred Oracle. These two words must become our life's mission. To "Know Thyself" means, in this context, to recognize our relationship persona and release it, for as Krishnamurti said, "Before we can have any relationship with another...it is essential that we begin to understand ourselves first."

The next chapter is devoted to aiding you in this process. I'm going to share the full story behind my relationship persona and how it played out in my relationship with my ex fiancée. It will serve as both a model and an inspiration of how your effort to "Know Thyself" can dramatically change your love life and end The Relationship Groundhog Day Syndrome.

Attraction Factors

1. Describe the type of person you seem to attract.

2. Describe the pattern your relationships seem to take, your version of Groundhog Day.

3. Based upon the types of people and patterns you attract, what persona or role must you be playing in your love life?

— 16 —

A Little Ditty About Roy and Julie

"In the early stages of many so-called romantic relationships, role-playing is quite common in order to attract and keep whoever is perceived by the ego as the one who is going to 'make me happy, make me feel special, and fulfill all my needs.' 'I'll play who you want me to be, and you'll play who I want you to be.' That's the unspoken and unconscious agreement. However, role-playing is hard work, and so those roles cannot be sustained indefinitely, especially once you start living together."

~ Eckhart Tolle

One of John Mellencamp's most famous songs is, *A Little Ditty About Jack and Diane.*[32] It's a story of two American kids growing up in the heartland. Well, in like fashion, I'd like to share a little ditty about "Casanova"[33] (the actual name of "Roy the Rescuer") and my ex fiancée, "Damsel" (Julie). We were two American kids growing up in suburbs of Chicago.

In order to help you "Know Thyself" and understand how personas work in the attraction phase of a relationship, I'm going tell you a bit about our backgrounds, how we met and the relationship we created together.

"Casanovas" Story

I became "Casanova" when I was about 7 years old in order to be emotionally close to my mother. While she never missed one of my sporting events and took care of all my family's physical needs, she was perfectionistic, emotionally cold and demanding. If you wanted to be close to her, you did it her way. You did not want to piss her off. If you did, you would get the fuming, silent treatment. To this day, I can still hear my dad's voice: "Son, don't piss her off. I know what you want and it doesn't matter. Just do it her way. Make her happy. It's just not worth it."

---

[32] Enjoy. http://bit.ly/1hHV6BG

[33] At the risk of confusing you, from this point forward, I'm changing the name of "Roy the Rescuer" to his formal name of "Casanova", who was a notorious ladies man back in the 18th century. "Casanova" better describes how I functioned in relationships and it's best to not use your real name, because, after all, the persona is not really you.

Like any child, I wanted to be emotionally close to my mom. I wanted to feel her love. So I tried to be a good little boy, one that pleased her, did what she wanted and made her life better. I laid aside my wants and needs, and instead, did whatever it took to make her happy. And when I did that, WOW, I felt her love! She was warm and emotionally available. But every once in a while, if I lost sight of her agenda and did my own thing, she'd become angry, cold and distant. I'd lose my connection to her.

What I learned from my relationship with my mom, my first girlfriend you could say, was that if I wanted the attention and affection of a woman, I had to be a "good boy." In other words, in order to be close and connected to a woman, my life had to be about taking care of hers. This was my "shape," my relationship persona, my way of relating to women. I came to believe that I had to be "Casanova" if I wanted a woman to love me.

Now, let me tell you how Julie developed her "shape" as "Damsel."

"Damsel's" Story

Julie grew up feeling isolated and left to fend for herself. As a consequence, she became a very self-reliant and independent little girl. Her parents loved her, of course, but Julie never felt like anyone's priority, especially her father's. He worked a lot and when he was home, he was the strong, silent, stoic type. Suffice it to say, Julie never felt like "daddy's little girl." In fact, she would later tell "Casanova" that she had never been the center of any man's attention.

Her self-reliant attitude enabled her to earn degrees in Chemistry and Business Management, and after graduation she landed a demanding, high-paying job. Partly because of her ambition, but also because she was a single mother and the sole provider for two young boys, Julie consistently chose to work 60-80 hours a week, including nights and weekends. So, when "Casanova" met her, she was overwhelmed with responsibilities. Life was crazy. Managing her demanding career, raising her two boys and running her household left her with hardly any time to breathe.

Julie's "shape," or relationship persona, therefore, was that of a lonely "damsel in distress." She was overwhelmed with responsibility and had never been the priority in a man's life.

"Casanova" Meets "Damsel"

"Two personas walk into a bar..." That might be the way this little ditty would go if it were a joke, but it's not. We actually did meet in a bar, a swanky placed called, *The Clubhouse*. The details of the evening aren't important.[34] All you need to know is that we immediately hit it off. In fact, that's an understatement. It was the closest thing to love at first sight that I've ever experienced. The attraction and chemistry was instant, and it's obvious as to why, isn't it? We were a perfect match.

I walked into the bar as "Casanova," a guy who thought the only way to get a woman to want him was to take care of her every need. "Damsel" came in overwhelmed by her lifestyle and disappointed that she'd never been a man's priority.

Were there ever two personas that were better suited for one another? Two weeks into our relationship, "Damsel" half-jokingly said, "I don't expect to be a man's top priority, only somewhere in his top 10." Well, this was her lucky day! "Damsel" wouldn't be *in* the top 10; she'd *BE* the top 10! "Casanova" was built to make a woman the absolute focal point of his entire life. In fact, he doesn't know any other way to relate to a woman other than by spoiling the hell out of her.

We were like cookies and milk.

Falling In Love

I know this will sound cynical, but falling in love is nothing more than two perfectly matched puzzle pieces meeting one another. By the end of our second date we fell in love. Hard. How could we not? We complimented each other perfectly.

"Casanova" was so incredibly enamored with "Damsel" that he outdid himself. Knowing how overwhelmed she was with her demanding career, he relieved her of any duties around the house. He began doing her entire family's laundry. He made the beds, straightened up the boy's rooms and took care of her dog, a yellow Lab. He had her house professionally cleaned on a regular basis, washed her car and even mowed her lawn.

He also stepped in and took over the parenting responsibilities. He got the kids up, fed them and took them to school. Even though he had his own full time job as a professional golfer and instructor, he picked the kids up from school, helped them with their homework, took them to tutoring appointments and to their sporting events.

When "Damsel" came home after her normal 13-hour day, he'd run interference between her and the boys so she could decompress. He'd regular-

---

[34] The details of this entire relationship are covered in *Relationship Addiction—A Memoir,* my first book.

ly massage the knots out of her neck and shoulders and help her process the challenges she faced at work.

So, within two weeks, "Casanova" was "Damsel's" maid, nanny, Masseuse, coach and parent of her children. Nothing like this had ever happened to "Damsel" before. She was the absolute center of a man's attention. She was being spoiled rotten and swept off her feet. She didn't have to worry about anything. "Casanova" had come to the rescue. She, of course, fell madly in love with him, and every morning and every night, she expressed her love sexually. In fact, she wore "Casanova" out.

In this sense, "Casanovas" dream was coming true, too. He was taking care of her life, and damn, was she ever taking care of his! Almost every moment of their relationship was spent in bed. (Hell, there wasn't anything else for her to do!)

The Inevitable

Now, you might be wondering, "Well, what's wrong with that, Roy? You're taking care of her and she's taking care of you. Everybody's happy. Where's the problem?"

Well, there wasn't a problem, not as long as both of us continued to play our roles. But as Eckhart Tolle said in the quote that opened this chapter, "role-playing is hard work, and so those roles cannot be sustained indefinitely." Eventually and inevitably, "The Law of P's" is going to kick in:

Personas > Playmates > Patterns > Problems > Pain

When we're relating as a *persona*, we always attract a *playmate* with a matching "shape." The relationship then follows a familiar *pattern*, and that inevitably results in *problems* and eventually *pain*. If you look closely, you'll see that this has been the story of your life. I know it was mine. Let me tell you how "Casanova" and "Damsel" fell apart. It illustrates the way all persona relationships go.

Trouble In Paradise

Whenever a persona attracts its playmate, an unconscious and very conditional agreement is at the core of the relationship. It's never recognized as such, but the agreement is, "I'll be my persona IF you'll be yours." So, for "Casanova" and "Damsel," it was this: I would take care of her life—IF—she'd take care of mine, and vice versa. Notice, though, that if either of us stopped playing our roles, we'd no longer match. Our puzzle pieces wouldn't fit together. Instead of being cookies and milk, we'd be cookies and, say, tomato juice. Yuck.

That's what happened to us. Once we got engaged, Tolle's prediction came true. I got tired of being "Casanova". I didn't want to be her maid and nanny. Yes, I wanted to participate in our relationship, but I got tired of playing my rescuing role.

And on a deeper level, everything I had been doing was driven by fear. It's very important to recognize that every relationship persona is 100% fear-driven. There's nothing loving and authentic about them. No matter how sweet and sincere they seem, they are expressions of a fearful heart. And nothing is sustainable when it's driven by fear.

Raising Julie's kids and running her household were not authentic expressions of love. They were things I did because I was scared. I was unconsciously running my mommy script. I thought I had to be a "good boy" in order to get Julie (or any woman) to want me. In other words, "Casanova" existed for a purpose, which was to get a woman to love and want him, and now that "Damsel" did, "Casanova" was no longer necessary.

So, as I began expressing my displeasure about our lifestyle and suggested we make some changes, our relationship went on "tilt." It didn't work anymore. We were now cookies and tomato juice. We started to make each other miserable and Julie ended our relationship.

The Ditty's Danger

The danger in telling you this "little ditty" is that because it seems so extreme, you might not be able to relate to it. You might think, "Wow, Roy, that's pretty messed up. I'm not doing anything like *that*." Here's what I want to say to you:

Oh yes you are.

Don't kid yourself. You are doing *exactly* that. You just don't see it yet. You're doing something just as "extreme," though most likely in a different way. Your work is to "Know Thyself," and you're half way there because the last chapter helped you identify your "shape." Now, as we conclude this chapter, it's time for you to expand your awareness beyond your "shape," and write your own "little ditty" about how your persona has played itself out in real life. The goal is to see your relationship history as clearly as I see mine. Once you do that, then you're ready to de-construct your relationship persona, or as I like to call it, "shape-shift." That is where we turn our attention now.

Attraction Factors

1. Write your own little ditty about how your persona-self shows up in real life. It does not have to be about a long-term relationship. It can be about how you never get a second date, for example. Simply describe your persona, along with your playmate's, then describe the pattern you experience and the problems and pain it creates.

2. Extra Credit: Do you notice your persona-self showing up in areas beyond your love life? Perhaps in your career or in the way you relate to your friends or family members? (Hint: It is. You just have to see it.)

— 17 —

Shape-Shifting

"What you resist, persists."

~ Carl Jung

The premise of this section of the book is that if we want to attract our ideal partner and create a lasting relationship with them, we must recognize and release our relationship personas. This "shape," this false and fear-driven way of relating is one of the seven major barriers we've built against love, and it leads to attracting the same kinds of playmates, patterns, problems and pain over and over again. Our "shapes" must be shifted so that a more authentic and healthy way of being in a relationship can emerge.

The question is, how do we do that? For example, how do I stop being "Casanova" and how do you stop being whatever persona has you in its grip? Well, at the risk of being overly simplistic, there is a conventional approach and a conscious approach to shape-shifting.

Friend or Foe?

The conventional approach is about making an enemy out of whatever you want to change—in this case, a relationship persona. It says that if you can muster up enough anger and hatred toward something, if you are willing to fight, or even loathe the part of your life that needs changing, then that resistance will generate the necessary willpower, determination and effort it takes to change. This is, "The war on (blank)," approach.

Weight loss is a perfect example. We could say it's "The war on your body." Conventional wisdom says that the more anger and hatred you have for your body, the more motivated you'll be to change your eating and exercise habits. So, the conventional approach can be best summed up by the word: *resistance*.

The conscious approach, however, is the complete opposite. It says, "What you resist, persists," or "What you fight against, you strengthen." If you want to change some aspect of your life, especially a way of relating, the conscious approach says don't make an enemy of it. Don't hate it or yourself for doing it. Instead, welcome and even embrace your relationship persona. Resisting will only strengthen its hold on you. So, in other words, make it your friend. The conscious approach says not to run away from that which you want to change, run toward it and embrace it.

Hating "Casanova"

When I first became aware of "Casanova", I hated him. He made me sick. I was embarrassed, ashamed and disgusted with my "shape." The last thing I wanted to do was move toward "Casanova" and embrace him. Frankly, that sounded like new age, psychobabble bullshit and a waste of time. "Casanova" was my enemy and I wanted to get rid of him.

My guess is you feel the same way. You are probably sick and tired of your persona and the damage it's caused. You'd like to get rid of it too. I understand, but it won't work. You can't grit your teeth and resist your way out of a persona, because what you resist, persists. So, rather than resisting, hating and rejecting our personas, we must choose to move towards them, and embrace them with a loving, playful spirit.

If that boggles your mind, I get it. This is a radical, counter-intuitive way of approaching life change. However, the cool thing about the conscious approach is that you don't have to believe it. You don't have to convince yourself of it or even have faith in it. None of that is necessary. *All you have to do is try it.* The proof, as they say, is in the pudding.

Just Do It!

I'm going to share 7 very practical and doable steps on how to embrace your relationship persona and break free from The Relationship Groundhog Day Syndrome once and for all. However, you can't just read about them; *you have to DO them.* As the Nike slogan says, "Just Do It." If you merely read these 7 steps and move on to the next chapter, nothing will change. Knowing your "shape" is important, but it's not enough. Awareness is only part of it. Do not delude yourself here. Without actually doing the following 7 steps, Groundhog Day will never end.

The 7 Steps of Shape-Shifting

Before we jump into the 7 Steps, a couple of preliminary comments are in order.

First, I want to invite you to approach them, as I said a minute ago, with a playful spirit. Have fun with these steps. In fact, your ability to laugh and see the humor in your persona is *THE* evidence that its hold on your life is broken. If you're serious and bunched up with this, you're resisting. However, if you're light and playful around these steps, you're embracing.

Secondly, there is an increasing level of difficulty, or challenge, as you work through the steps, meaning, Step 1 is the easiest and Step 7 is the hardest. Additionally, each step builds on the previous one. You won't be able to do Step 2 without doing Step 1 first, and that's true of all of them. So they must be done in order.

Third, the power of the steps is in their cumulative effect. They are synergistic; meaning, the sum of the steps is greater than any individual step. In other words, for the most profound relationship change, do them all.

Now we're ready for the 7 Steps. I'll cover the first six in this chapter and Step 7 in the next.

Step 1: Epithet

The first step is to name your relationship persona. An *Epithet* is a word or phrase used to describe an actual or attributed quality in a person. "Casanova", or "Debbie the Damsel," are examples.

This is a very important step. A persona's power comes from its ability to operate unconsciously in the background of our lives, masquerading as our authentic self. By naming the persona, however, we bring it out of the darkness and expose it, thereby putting a little space between it and us. This begins the releasing process.

Let me give you a couple of pointers on picking a good Epithet, or name.

a) It's critical to NOT use your real name. A few chapters back, I spoke of, "Roy the Rescuer", and I did so only to help you understand personas and how they work. But it's best not to use your name because it strengthens the sense that the persona is who you are. It's not. It's just some weird childhood coping mechanism run amok. So, for me, "Casanova" is a much better choice.

b) Choose a name that needs little or no explanation. "Donna the Doormat", "Suzy the Slut", or "Casanova", are epithets most people would understand easily.

c) Be as creative and playful as possible when choosing a name. Ideally, choose a name that comes from TV, movie, cartoon or fairy tale characters. Historical or even infamous people from politics, sports or religion are good too.

110

d) The name should perfectly capture the way the persona acts or functions in relationship. It's not who you want to be; it's who you want to stop being.

e) Feel free to use alliterations like "Suzy the Slut," or "Sam the Stalker," if you can't come up with anything more creative.

f) Create your own word, if need be. When I have a female client who will settle for anything she can get, we'll use, "Crumbgirl," because she'll take whatever falls off the table.

g) Lastly, feel free to make up an entire phrase. My wife has a persona that I named, "Little-Ms.-I-don't-want-to-be-a-bother," because when she's caught in that trance, she doesn't value herself and won't ask for help.

Step 2: Explain

Step 2 is to write a very concise, one sentence description that *explains* how your persona operates. In other words, describe its M.O. (method of operation). In my case, it would be, "Casanova prioritizes women and ignores himself, so that he can get a woman's attention and affection."

To help you write yours, here are a couple of examples.

- **"Suzy the Slut"** chooses to be sexual very early in a relationship so that she can control men and get them to love her.
- **"Donna the Doormat"** can't say "no," or stand up for herself, so that she can avoid conflict and feel safe.
- **"Freddie the Fireman"** (a persona similar to "Casanova") responds to emergencies and rescues others so that he can get approval and feel special.
- **"George"** (as in George Costanza) never approaches women so that he can avoid being hurt and rejected.
- **"Nancy the Nurse"** takes care of broken down men so that she can feel needed and loved.
- **"Crumbgirl"** settles for what she can get or stays in unhealthy relationships so that she can avoid feeling abandoned and lonely.

Notice each explanation has three basic parts: (1) The name, (2) The behavior, and (3) The goal. Write yours in the same way. Do not include your story about where the persona came from or who's to blame for it. All that matters is what's happening now. Take ownership of it and simply describe its M.O.

111

Step 3: Examine

Now that you've named your persona and described how it operates, the real welcoming and embracing can begin. I want you to interview, or *examine* your relationship persona. This step is about getting to know the persona intimately and allowing it to tell you its innermost wants, needs, feelings and fears.

This is the conscious approach in action. We are not trying to get rid of the persona or resist it; we're actually inviting it to come forward, to have it take center stage and to allow it to be seen, heard and *appreciated*. We're embracing the persona.

The best way to examine the persona is to ask a trusted friend to interview you—*as the persona*. In other words, get "in character," if you will, and become the persona. Fully embody it, which might mean putting your body in a certain position, taking on a facial expression and even altering your voice. Be the persona. Really get into it, go all the way with this.

The interviewer's role is to ask you six questions, but in so doing, they must address you *by the persona's name*, not your real name. The real you doesn't exist right now. So, for example, if you were interviewing me, the first question would be, *"Casanova"*, what's the most important thing to you?" Each question would start with your persona's name. And the answers would be given "in character." "Casanova" would answer with his perspective, his feelings, his desires, his fears. *Answer as the persona*. Do not speak about how you should feel or what you want to feel. Speak as the persona, and be REAL. Do not try to sound healthy or evolved.

Here are the six questions:

1. _____, what's the most important thing to you?
2. _____, what are you most proud of?
3. _____, when did you make your first appearance?
4. _____, who did you learn your style from?
5. _____, what are you most afraid of?
6. _____, what do you most want?

Step 4: Example

After naming, describing and interviewing your persona, you should have a pretty good understanding of the "person" you become in order to get attention, affection, approval or applause in relationships.

However, it's easy to fall back under its spell. Remember, personas are very old, habitual ways of relating, and therefore, they're hard to break.

You will "fall asleep," and find yourself being that "person" again. So, how can you "stay awake" and keep yourself from drifting back into old patterns?

That's where Step 4 comes in. This step is to find a *physical example* of your persona, something that will remind you of its tendencies every time you see it or touch it. This is a very powerful and effective way to "stay awake" and not drift back into old, unconscious habits.

Back when I was first coming to terms with "Casanova", it was literally three steps forward, two steps back. I can't tell you the number of times I found myself being "him" again. In fact, I usually didn't even know I was doing it until my friends or my coach, Diana, pointed it out. "Casanova" was such an ingrained habit in me, that without even knowing it, I'd slip back into being "him." And you will too. So you need to get something that physically reminds you of your persona, so that doesn't happen.

My coach told me to get a cigarette lighter and carry it in my pocket. I didn't smoke and neither did the women I dated, but she said that didn't matter. The lighter would serve as a physical example of being the kind of guy who is always ready to meet his woman's needs. She told me that every time I felt it in my pocket, it would remind me to not fall back under "Casanova's" spell. That's brilliant, isn't it?

I want you to do the same thing. Find a physical item that represents your persona, but it has to be something funny *and* something that you regularly come in contact with. The lighter made me chuckle and it was right there in my pocket. That's perfect.

Items that can go on your keychain, or purse strap, or something that can hang from your rear view mirror or fit in your pocket are ideal. A picture on your refrigerator or bathroom mirror is good, as are pictures on the desktop of your computer or cell phone. Whatever it is, make it fun and something you bump into all the time.

Here are some examples based on the personas I listed in Step 2:

- **"Suzy the Slut"**—Get a bracelet, or a keychain, that has the name "Suzy" on it. (This is a good thing to do for any persona.) Or, if you want to be more radical and more fun, download a picture of a famous porn star, frame it and put it on your nightstand. How do you jump in the sack with some guy you just met when that picture is staring at you?
- **"Donna the Doormat"**—Get an actual doormat, or even a car floor mat, and have "Donna" put on it. Or, you could even cut a small piece of rubber off an actual doormat, punch a hole in it and

put it on your key chain. Or, one of the Monopoly pieces was the "shoe." Hang it off your rear view mirror.

- **"Freddie the Fireman"**—Go to *Toys R Us* and get a little red fire truck and put it in your car's cup holder or hang it from your rear view mirror. (What a great conversation piece for a first date!) You could also get a plastic fireman's hat and put it your mantel.
- **"George Costanza"**—Get his picture and put it on your fridge or bathroom mirror, or better yet, put it in your wallet so that you see his face every time you open it. People will see it and you'll have to explain! Perfect.
- **"Nancy the Nurse"**—Get a picture of *Florence Nightingale* and put it where you'll see it all the time. Or, get a stethoscope or a blood pressure cuff and hang it around your bathroom doorknob or even your rear view mirror. A little cute nurses hat would be good too. You could try it on before you go on a date or to a single's event. (Do you see how fun this can be?)
- **"Crumbgirl"**—Get the smallest container of bread crumbs you can from the grocery store, empty it and put it in your car's cup holder or purse. In fact, get a bunch of them and put them all over your house. If you work in an office, put one on your desk!

Step 5: Expose

Step 5 is to *expose* your persona by going public about it. This is based on the Biblical wisdom that says, "Confess your sins and you shall be healed."

When I recognized I was being "Casanova" with women, I immediately went to my closest guy friends and told them all about "him." I told them how I took care of a woman's every need—and lost myself—all in an effort to get her to love me. Once I had explained "Casanova", I asked my friends if they would be willing to do whatever it took to wake me up if (or more likely when) they ever saw me being "Casanova". I knew it was easy to fall back under his spell and I needed my friends to hold me accountable.

Step 5, then, is to go public with your persona by telling your close friends about your unhealthy way of relating and asking them to call you out when they see you stuck in its trance.

But that's only the beginning. There's another part to Step 5 and it's really, really scary. You must expose your persona to the very people you're most likely to use it on—*the people you date!* As outrageous as it sounds, you must go public about your persona to your partners. If you "out" yourself and tell them about your persona, how it operates and what it's after, how could you still do it with them?

114

I told my wife, MaryMargaret, about "Casanova" on about our third date. Why? *Because I really didn't want to relate as "him" anymore.* I didn't want this relationship to go the way all the others had. So I told her about how I had a history of being this really nice guy, the world's greatest boyfriend. I told her how I would take care of everything in a woman's life, not because I want to or because I loved her, but because I was afraid a woman would never love me if I didn't.

As you can imagine, that was not easy to say and it probably scares the hell out of you. I know this idea is pretty incredible. But do you want to break free of the Groundhog Day Syndrome or not? If you keep quiet, you're likely to repeat your relationship history—AGAIN! Is that what you want? How committed are you to a new, healthier kind of relationship? This is the cutting edge of conscious relationships. How much do you want to attract lasting love?

Now, I would advise you NOT to talk about this on a first date. "Hey, would you pass the salt, and by the way, I want you to know that I'm "Nancy the Nurse," and I look for men who are broken down and wounded so that I can feel loved and needed." Don't do that. It's a little much for a first date. But the question remains: When should you expose your persona to someone you're dating?

Well, certainly before you sleep with them. That's a significant milestone and if you want to keep this new relationship from turning out like all the rest, it's best to expose your persona before your relationship becomes sexual.

Step 6: Exaggerate

The sixth step to releasing a relationship persona is to make it bigger, to *exaggerate* the persona to such an extent that the whole thing becomes hilarious.

Let's face it. When you step back and look at the crazy things you do for love, it's pretty funny isn't it? I mean, think of my life. I meet this woman and within a couple of weeks I'm washing her kids socks and folding her laundry! Come on. That's sick, but hilarious.

When you become aware of your persona AND find it hysterically funny, that's when you know it no longer has a grip on your life. And exaggeration does that. So Step 6 is about becoming outrageously playful and dramatic with our personas. Again, this is the opposite of resisting. This is uber-embracing. We're playing with them, acting them out in big, hilarious ways.

It took me a while before I was able to do this, however. Like I said earlier, I hated "Casanova" for a long time. He was needy and desperate and I wanted to get rid of him. But after a while, I let go of my self-loathing and I began to see the humor in him. I mean, I thought I had to be a woman's maid, nanny and Masseuse to get her to want me. That's crazy and funny.

Are you at this point yet? Can you laugh at your relationship persona and the crazy stuff it does for love? Is "Crumbgirl," "Debbie the Doormat," "Freddie the Fireman," or whatever your persona is, funny to you? If not, that's all right. You have to work through Steps 1-5 first in order to see the humor of it all. And when you can, your "shape" has shifted.

When I felt "Casanova" was beginning to show up in my love life again, I would call my coach, *in character*, and exaggerate him. When she answered the phone, I would not say, "Hey Diana, it's Roy. I want to exaggerate "Casanova" with you. Are you up for that?" Instead, she'd answer and I would just start in *AS* "Casanova". No introductions, no explanations. My voice would be very sweet, sing-songy and romantic.

> *"Hello?"*

> *"Oh, Diana, you're the most wonderful coach in the whole wide world. You're so smart and enlightened! Oh my God, Diana, where would I be without you? Is there anything I can do for you? I am going to fly out to California and do your laundry and take care of your kids. I can be there in a few hours. Maybe you need a back rub too because I know how rough your life is. I can't wait to drop what I'm doing and come take care of you."*

She would immediately know what I was doing and play along:

> *"Oh, "Casanova", I neeeeeeeeeed you! Life is so tough right now. I'm exhausted and overwhelmed. The kids are driving me crazy and the house is a wreck. There's laundry piled up all over the floor and the fridge is empty. Could you come save me, "Casanova"? Could you come rescue me in my distress? I'm helpless and I can't survive without you! Oh, "Casanova", come quick and take care of me and I'll have sex with you all night long."*

By the end we'd both be laughing hysterically. "Casanova" is a riot, but more importantly, by exaggerating and making "him" bigger, its spell over me is broken. How could I turn around and be "Casanova" with some woman after that? There's no way.

Here's another example of Step 6 in action.

I recently spoke to a 50-year old woman who has a pattern of attracting men who don't show much interest in her. She told me that her latest boy-friend will occasionally invite her over to his house to watch a movie and have sex, but he doesn't take her anywhere or do anything special with her. That's the "shape" she's attracting, a persona I might call "Disinterested Danny." He's a guy that doesn't put much effort into a relationship.

Now, she must have a matching "shape," right? She must have a perso-na that fits with "Disinterested Danny." Sure enough, she does. Here is a sentence from an email she sent. See if you can spot her persona.

"I want him to know that I am a low maintenance girl when it comes to dating. I don't expect lots of big dates."

Do you see "her"? I'd call her "Low Maintenance Lucy." She fits per-fectly with "Disinterested Danny." She doesn't want to be a hassle. She's easy to date because she doesn't expect anything big or special. Underneath this persona, of course, is a deeply scared woman who doesn't value herself or feel worthy of love. For fun, let's do a case study and follow "Low Maintenance Lucy" through the first six steps.

Case Study

Step 1: Epithet—We've already got that. "Low Maintenance Lucy."

Step 2: Explain—"Low Maintenance Lucy" is an easy-going, hassle-free girlfriend who doesn't expect much so that she can keep her man's in-terest and not be alone.

Step 3: Examine—We would interview LML, asking her the six ques-tions.

Step 4: Example—I'd have her get a picture of *Lucille Ball* and hang it on her bathroom mirror or I'd have her go to *Toys R Us* and get a miniature wrench or screwdriver and hang it from her rear view mirror. (The small tool would signify that it doesn't take much to maintain her.)

Step 5: Expose—I'd have her invite her best girlfriends to happy hour and tell them all about "Low Maintenance Lucy." Every gory detail of how she settles for "Disinterested Danny" types and how she's so afraid to be a hassle or to own her value as a woman. Then I'd want her to formally invite her girlfriends to call her out whenever they see any expression of "Lucy."

Finally, I'd want her to tell "Disinterested Danny" all about "Low Maintenance Lucy" and that as of this moment, she's committed to being a high maintenance girlfriend, one that's going to require a lot of effort on his part, and if he's not willing to step up, she'd find someone else who is. (BOOM!)

Step 6: Exaggerate—I would instruct her that the next time she feels "Low Maintenance Lucy" coming on within herself or in a relationship with a guy, she's to call me, *in character as Lucy,* and exaggerate the persona. Speaking in a really whiny, begging, pleading, lonely little girl voice, I'd want her to say something like:

> *"Hi Danny. Could I please, please, please come over and just sit around with you? I won't ask anything of you and I certainly don't want to go anywhere and do anything. I promise not to be any trouble. Really, you won't even notice I'm there. I'll be good. I promise not to want anything more than to cook for you and have sex. That's it. I won't be any trouble. In fact, you don't even have to talk to me. You can be totally disinterested in me, as you always are. It's all right. I'll be really low maintenance. Can I please come over?"*

I would respond as "Disinterested Danny," saying:

> *"Who's this? Oh, it's you. I forgot we were dating. You want to come over? Geez, I don't know. I'm in not in the mood for any high maintenance bullshit. I'm tired and I want to stay home. If you come over, don't expect anything. I want to watch a movie and get a blowjob. Maybe you could even make me a sandwich. But one thing's for sure. We aren't going anywhere. I'm not taking you to any fancy place like the Olive Garden. You're just not worth the effort and I don't like you all that much anyway."*

Now, if this client had done Steps 1-5, that would be hilarious. We'd be rolling on the floor laughing about that because that's how she's lived. And it's crazy-funny. How could she then go into the dating scene and get caught in the grip of "Low Maintenance Lucy"? There's no way. The persona is broken; its grip on her life released.

118

Attraction Factors

1. Write your persona's name and one sentence description now.

2. What physical example are you going to get that represents your persona?

3. What friends or family members are you going to tell about your persona and request that they hold you accountable, and even call you out, whenever they see you caught in its grip?

Persona Parties

"Everyone is a moon and has a dark side,
which he never shows to anybody."

~ Mark Twain

Perhaps you're familiar with extreme workout programs like *P90X* or *CrossFit*. While they appeal to the insane fitness fanatic, they also produce the most dramatic results. I've done P90X a number of times, because, well, I'm insane.

The field of conscious relationships has something similar, a spiritual practice that is pretty insane itself, but it too, delivers dramatic results. It's called a Persona Party, and it's so fun and transformative that it deserves its own chapter. But before I explain it, let's reset the context.

I've been saying that our relationship persona, or emotional "shape," is one of the 7 major barriers to attracting lasting love. It is the reason behind The Relationship Groundhog Day Syndrome, the bizarre experience of attracting the same playmates, patterns, problems and pain over and over again.

If we ever wish to have a healthy, lasting relationship we have to release this persona, or "shape-shift" as I call it, and we do that by playfully doing the following 7 steps:

1. Epithet—name the persona
2. Explain—describe the persona's behavior
3. Examine—interview the persona
4. Example—find a physical representation of the persona
5. Expose—go public about the persona
6. Exaggerate—make the persona bigger
7. Embody—be the persona at a party

Having already covered the first six, we now turn our attention to Step 7, Persona Parties, which has a special appeal to those of us who are fanatical about creating conscious, fulfilling relationships.

Step 7: Embody

Do you remember the movie, *The Perfect Storm*, starring George Clooney?[35] It was the story of how two smaller weather systems combined to form one awesomely potent super storm. Step 7 is like that. It combines Steps 5 and 6 into one potent persona practice.

Step 5, you'll remember, was about exposing your persona publically, while Step 6 was about exaggerating it. Step 7, then, combines them into the perfect storm. We *embody* the persona by exaggerating it publically.

Halloween is a perfect opportunity to do this. If you want to fully release your relationship persona, turn your Halloween party into a persona party. Make it a party with a purpose.

Instead of everyone dressing up in random costumes, everyone dresses up as their persona. Everyone goes to the party in character, dressing like it, acting like it, talking like it—the whole nine yards. Furthermore, everyone stays in character for most of the night. This is outrageously fun and transformative. Here are a couple of random examples to inspire you.

- **"Suzy the Slut"**—Her costume would be to dress like a hooker. At the party, "Suzy" would walk up to men and say, "Hi there, big boy, I'm 'Suzy the Slut,' and I'm so desperate for a man to love me, that I'll do anything you want if you'll promise to always love me and never leave me."
- **"Donna the Doormat"**—Her costume would be a simple white tee shirt and she'd bring a big container of mud with her to the party. "Donna" would approach men and say, "Hey, my name is 'Donna the Doormat' and I like it when men walk all over me." Then, she'd lather the mud on the bottom of his shoe, lay on the floor and let him step on her!
- **"Freddie the Fireman"**—He would, of course, dress up as a fireman, and he'd approach women saying, "Hey baby, I'm 'Freddie the Fireman.' I feel so lonely and useless as a man that I will be available, at a moment's notice, to respond to any emergency you have, in hopes that you might think I'm a really nice guy and never dump me. Just dial 1-800-F-R-E-D-D-I-E and I'll be there in minutes, no matter what I'm doing, because maybe, just maybe, you'll love me and keep me around.

---

[35] Here's the trailer. http://bit.ly/1wYzndj

If you embrace your persona in these outrageous and playful ways, how could you possibly continue to relate like that? Wouldn't your "shape" have to change?

Now, if you're really certifiable, like my friends and I are, then you won't wait for Halloween. You can create (or attend) your own Persona Party. I went to such a party at my coach's home in Santa Cruz, California, back in 2012. I was there with 35 coaches for a weekend workshop. Let me give you some backstory before I tell you what happened.

By 2012, "Casanova" rarely showed up in my love life anymore. I had long since let "him" go when it came to my relationships with women, including my wife. But as I mentioned earlier, these personas often appear in other areas of our lives too. They're not restricted to our relationships. This was true in my situation. In the months before this Persona Party, I had recognized that I was being "Casanova" *in my coaching practice.*

Just as "Relationship Casanova" would do anything for a woman to get her to love him, so "Coach Casanova" would do anything to get a client to hire him.

The same fear-based M.O. had simply shifted from one area of my life to another! For example, I was so desperate for clients that I'd do anything to keep them, including drastically reducing my fees, sometimes by more than 50%! There were times where I'd let them set their own fees and pay me whatever they wanted. I'd do anything to get them to work with me. If a client couldn't pay at all, "Coach Casanova" would let them pay later, or tell them to take care of it whenever they could. If local clients didn't want to drive to my office for their sessions, "Coach Casanova" would drive to them, which was sometimes a two-hour round trip. And, of course, "Coach Casanova" would never charge them for gas or the extra time. They might "break up" with him if he did that!

Do you get the picture? I would do anything to get or keep clients, just like I would do anything to get and keep a woman.

It dawned on me that I was a whore!
I would do anything for a dollar.

Just as I degraded myself to get a woman's attention and affection, now I was degrading myself to get a client's "attention and affection." It was the same damn pattern, and it was happening with client after client after client. *I was experiencing Groundhog Day in my coaching practice!*

I was horrified when I recognized this. But I knew exactly what to do. I followed Steps 1-6 immediately, and when I went to California, I used the Persona Party my coach was throwing to work through Step 7.

Since I felt like a whore who degraded himself for money, I did something outrageous at this party. I went wearing literally nothing but a leopard striped G-string and long trench coat. To complete the ensemble, and to let the other partiers know what persona I was embodying, I made a sign that I wore around my neck. It said, "Will Be Degraded For Money."

Now see if you can picture this: I am in a room full of men and women dressed like a flasher. It got so hot, that the trench coat had to go. So I spent two hours running around the room in nothing but a G-string (totally sober, mind you), going to everyone with the same request: "I'm a whore who does anything for money. If you put a dollar in my G-string, I will do anything you ask."

Now, what makes for a good Persona Party is the willingness of each participant to support everyone else in whatever issue they're trying to release.[36] And, boy oh boy, did they ever support me! Everyone took turns degrading me. They put dollar bills in my G-string and told me to jump on the furniture and make monkey sounds; I was told to lick people's feet and someone even put a leash on me and made me follow them around on hands and knees like a dog. And it gets worse.

Someone went into Diana's kitchen and got a spatula. For a dollar, I bent over and let them smack my ass really hard. I mean *hard*. After each smack I had to say, "Yes! Degrade me more. I'll do anything for a dollar! (My ass was literally black and blue for a week.)

That wasn't enough, however. I was so insanely committed to releasing "Casanova's" hold on my any aspect of my life that I finally did degrading things—for free! Not even a dollar. (After all, I sometimes coached people for free.) Then, just to go completely off the deep end, I took the dollars I had received *and started paying people to degrade me!* "Please, I'll give *you* a dollar if you tell me to do something really nasty and degrading."

If you think I'm nuts, you're probably right. But I'm free of "Casanova". It was the most outrageous, hilarious and transformative night of my entire life. People were laughing so hard they were in tears. And I was too.

---

[36] This is critical. Everyone must understand the party's purpose and they must fully participate by embodying their persona too. Everyone must buy in.

(Well, my tears were a mixture of joy and pain.) This was *exactly* how I was living my life! I *was* degrading myself—first with women and now with clients. Yes, I was radically exaggerating things, but the fact of the matter was that I was living this way. At the party, I simply chose to be honest about it in a very public and hilarious way.

The results? Well, my dealings with clients have never been the same since. I no longer degrade myself and devalue myself in my coaching practice. My prices are my prices. Take it or leave it. I'm worth every penny I charge. "Casanova" is gone from my business, and it happened, not because I hated and resisted "him," but because I fully embraced "him" by exaggerating him publically.

I hope you are willing to do something similarly insane for yourself. Your life will never be the same, nor will your relationships. Groundhog Day will be over, once and for all.

Attraction Factors
1. In what ways, and in what situations, can you exaggerate your persona and make it bigger?

2. What's your plan for next Halloween?

BARRIER SIX

CHARACTER
Awakening Your Masculine or Feminine Essence

"If a man has a Masculine sexual essence, then his priority is his mission, his direction toward greater release, freedom, and consciousness. If a woman has a Feminine sexual essence, then her priority is the flow of love in her life, including her relationship with a man whom she can totally trust, in body, emotion, mind, and spirit. Man and woman must support each other in their priorities if the relationship is going to serve them both."

~ David Deida

When my son was 12, we went to *Grand Teton National Park,* in Wyoming, and hiked to *Lake Solitude,* which is 7.5 miles up the mountain. He was excited when we started, but as we approached our destination, he wasn't having fun anymore. It was hard work. He was exhausted.

I bet you can relate. You were probably excited when you began this book, but after the first five barriers, you're probably exhausted too. If so, I don't blame you. It has been hard work. But like I told my son, the hard part is over. From here on, our journey is "downhill" and way more fun.

With our personas recognized and released, we're now able to relate as our authentic Masculine or Feminine selves. But what does that mean? There is a lot of misunderstanding and misuse of these divine energies and that creates our sixth barrier. We must become masters of Masculine and Feminine dynamics if we want to attract lasting love and that is our task in this section. This is, by far, the longest (and most enjoyable) section of the book. Here's how it unfolds:

— 19 —

Two Kinds of Chemistry

"Most of us fall in love with someone's persona and spend the next three to five years discovering who that person really is."

~ Jennifer Aniston

A few chapters back, I made the provocative statement that the feeling we call "falling in love" happens when two perfectly matched personas meet one another and mistake their inevitable chemistry for love.

I realize that sounds pretty cynical, but that's exactly what happened when I walked into that bar in suburban Chicago and met my ex fiancée, Julie. My persona was "Casanova" and hers was "Damsel in Distress." We fit like cookies and milk. There was instant and profound chemistry and we fell madly in love with each other.

But it was not our authentic selves that fell in love with each other; it was our personas that fell in love with each other!

In other words, our chemistry was persona-based. Here is a staggering, counter-cultural insight:

Chemistry is a very dangerous and untrustworthy feeling.

I realize that probably doesn't sit well with you because chemistry is such a desirable and wonderful feeling. We all want to feel it. Our bodies literally come alive with sexual energy. When I first met "Damsel," I had never felt so happy and alive in all my life. I felt the kind of feelings that songwriters, poets and fairy-tales describe—*I had fallen in love.*

However, it wasn't me who had fallen in love; it was "Casanova". "He" had fallen for "Damsel," not me. So even though we all want to feel intense chemistry with another person, it's wise to be suspicious of it, *for who is actually feeling it?* Is it our authentic self or is it our persona?

Until you've recognized and released your relationship persona, chances are very high that it's your persona that feels chemistry and falls in love, not your deeper, authentic Masculine or Feminine self.

Persona Chemistry

Understanding persona-based chemistry will explain a lot of bizarre experiences in the dating scene. For example, have you ever met a really great person, someone you knew would make a great partner because they were nice looking, had a decent job and seemed honest and sincere, and yet you didn't feel any real attraction or chemistry towards them? It's strange, isn't it? On paper they're everything you want, and yet there's no juice, no sexual attraction. Why? Well, it's almost always because they're "shape" doesn't fit with yours. Your personas don't match.

Here are some examples:

- If you're "Debbie the Doormat," you will only feel chemistry with "Charley the Control Freak." If you happen to meet a healthy man, one who isn't controlling, there won't be any chemical attraction between the two of you because you're energetically incompatible.
- If you're "Suzy the Slut," you will only feel chemistry with "Joe the John," the guy who only wants only "one thing." But if you met a man who is actually interested in more than your body, neither of you will feel a spark.
- If you're "Freddie the Fireman," you will feel a lot of sexual attraction toward "Little Ms. 911," but when you meet a woman who can take care of herself, even if she's beautiful, you won't feel drawn to one another.
- If you're "Crumbgirl," you will feel strangely turned on by "Disinterested Danny," but when you meet a man who's truly emotionally available and ready for intimacy, you won't feel chemically drawn to him.

The best solution to end Persona Chemistry is, of course, to recognize and release your relationship personas by working through the 7 Steps outlined in the previous chapters. *When you do that work, you will find yourself attracted to a different type of person.* The types of people that used to make you yawn will now make you yearn (and vice versa). You'll pass on the "bad boy" type. He just won't do it for you anymore. "Damsels" will bore you. Broken down men won't turn you on, nor will the emotionally unavailable types. You'll be attracted to a whole new kind of person because, well, *you're a whole new person.*

When Your "Picker" is Broken

So, the first type of chemistry is *Persona Chemistry*. But before I describe the second kind of chemistry, something I call, *Polarity Chemistry*, I want to take a brief time-out and share a fun strategy that will help you if you feel your "picker" is broken.[37]

When my clients have found themselves living in Groundhog Day, habitually picking the wrong partners over and over again, I advise them to delegate the entire picking process to their close, trusted friends. In other words, if your "picker" is broken, *then don't pick.* Let your friends pick your partners for you.

For example, if you're dating online, give your friends access to your online account(s) and let them decide whom you should respond to or contact. When you're out with your friends on Saturday night, or after work, or even at some sort of event, let your friends determine who gets your number or whom you ask out.

If your "picker" is broken, take it out of the equation. Tell your friends that you don't trust yourself and that you will go out with whomever they think would be good for you.

Here's what will happen—I guarantee it. Your friends will choose someone and you'll say, "*Him?* No way! He seems nice, but I don't feel attracted to him," or "*Her?* Not a chance! She doesn't do it for me."

That's the point! Of course they don't do it for you. Your friends aren't picking with your persona! They don't have your "shape." Your close, trusted friends will pick the type of person that you *should* be attracted to, and frankly, they will pick the type of person, that in your essence, you *are* attracted to.

Now, if you don't want a man who's, say, 4 inches shorter than you, of course your friends won't pick a man like that. And if you don't want children, your buddies won't choose a single mother for you. So don't worry about being put with inappropriate people. Your friends know and love you and they won't do that to you.

But since they don't have your energetic wiring, they also won't pick players, damsels, control freaks or whatever type normally turns you on but leaves you hurt, empty and ultimately, single.

---

[37] For a complete discussion of this strategy, see my eCourse, *Dating in the Digital Age.*

Polarity Chemistry

The first type of chemistry is called, *Persona Chemistry*. It is dangerous and not to be trusted. But once we've worked through the 7 Steps, or even delegated the entire choosing process to our friends, that form of chemistry becomes a non-issue and the possibility of a more authentic kind of chemistry arises in its place. This is called *Polarity Chemistry*, better known as Masculine/Feminine chemistry.

Polarity is defined as "the presence of two opposite or contrasting principles or energies," and when it comes to relationships, these two opposite energies are Masculine and Feminine.

The leading voice on Masculine and Feminine dynamics is author, David Deida.[38] He writes:

> "Sexual attraction is based on sexual polarity, which is the force of passion that arcs between Masculine and Feminine poles. All natural forces flow between two poles. The North and South Poles of the Earth create a force of magnetism. The positive and negative poles of your electrical outlets or car battery create an electrical flow. In the same way, Masculine and Feminine poles between people create the flow of sexual feeling. This is sexual polarity."

The Friend Zone

But notice also that when two magnets are arranged so that the *same* poles come near each other—for instance, two north poles or two south poles—they repel each other. This explains the dreaded "Friend Zone." It happens when two of the same energies are brought near each other. There may be respect and even admiration, but there won't be any sexual attraction. If you find that people see you as a friend more than a lover, it's because you're animating the same energy they are. The guy feels like a "Girly-Man" and the woman feels like a "Tom-Boy." The solution is to reconnect to your deep Masculine or Feminine core, which is what this section is all about.

So, when we finally let go of our false, fear-driven personas, we're then able to relate authentically from either our Masculine or Feminine essence. The chemistry we experience is holy and healthy because we are aligned

---

[38] I will quote David Deida frequently throughout this section. His is book, <u>Intimate Communion: Awakening Your Sexual Essence</u>, is widely regarded as the standard when it comes to Masculine/Feminine dynamics. Almost all of my clients read it and I highly recommend it to you as well.

with our divine being-ness, rather than our childhood wounding. It is essential, therefore, that we learn about these two divine energies so that we can magnify them fully in our lives, for they are *THE* attraction factor in conscious, intimate relationships.

Energetic Confusion

However, as society has appropriately sought to rectify gender inequality, a terrible side-effect has happened: Men and women have become more and more sexually neutralized and androgynous, unable to give each other what they really want in intimacy. Deida writes:

> "I hear independent and successful women complaining that many of today's men have become "wimps," too weak and ambiguous to really trust, less committed to intimacy, and seemingly lost in their lives. Men are complaining that women are becoming hardened, more resistive and sharply independent. In short, men often ask me why women are becoming such "ballbusters" these days."

What he's saying is that men have been feminized and women have been masculinized and this depolarization has ruined *THE* attraction factor in relationships (and created the Friend Zone). So if we want to attract lasting love, we must first move beyond *Persona Chemistry*, then we have to master *Polarity Chemistry*, which means to reject societal pressure toward androgyny, and instead, unapologetically magnify our Masculine or Feminine sexual essence. And in the next few chapters, we are going to learn how to do just that.

Attraction Factors

1. What is your biggest learning from the discussion of Persona and Polarity Chemistry?

2. Are you willing to delegate the partner-picking process to your close, trusted friends, in order to avoid the dangerous effects of Persona-based Chemistry?

3. How would you define Masculine and Feminine energy and which one do you feel best represents your sexual essence?

20

Understanding Masculine and Feminine Energy

"In intimacy, when one partner's Masculine energy is brought near the other partner's Feminine energy, an attractive force of sexual polarity pulls them together."

~ David Deida

New York City is a place that feels driven, focused and structured. It's "the city that never sleeps," oozing purposeful energy that's all about overcoming obstacles, conquering the competition and achieving goals. New York City, in that regard, is a Masculine place.

Hawaii feels quite different. It's relaxing, renewing and nurturing. You don't go there to conquer the world, but to recover from it. Her energy is healing and rejuvenating. Hawaii is a Feminine place.

Just as places feel Masculine or Feminine, people do too. Those that love focusing on a project or competing against others to achieve their chosen mission are New York type people. They have a Masculine essence. *Their priority is where they're going and how they're going to get there.*

Conversely, those who feel happiest when they're connecting, conversing and communing with others, rather than competing against them, are Hawaii type people. They have a Feminine essence. *Their priority is not their direction, but the flow of love in their lives.*

These two energies are magnetically and powerfully attracted to each other. Just as two magnets are pulled together when their *opposite* north and south poles come near, so the Masculine and Feminine poles are pulled together when they come near each other. This is the basis of healthy chemistry in intimate relationships (as opposed to Persona Chemistry). When one partner's Masculine energy is brought near the other partner's Feminine energy, a magnetic force pulls them together. This force is called *Polarity Chemistry* and mastering it is the key to attracting lasting love.

Space and Stuff

However, these energies are reflections of something far deeper than mere geographical locations and personal preferences. They are reflections

132

of spiritual reality. They are "the two faces of God." Like a coin having two sides, so God, or the One Life, does too. Every major religious tradition teaches this. It's the apparent duality of the unseen and the seen. The Christian tradition calls it *Spirit and Flesh*.[39] Chinese philosophy calls it, *Yang and Yin*. Buddhism calls it, *Formlessness and Form*, or *Emptiness and Energy*. This duality is also called Masculine and Feminine.

To simplify things, I call the Masculine, *Space* (emptiness), and the Feminine, *Stuff* (energy), because if you look into the night sky, or even in the room in which you're now sitting, you'll see a bunch of *stuff*, be it stars or furniture, resting in, or being contained by, vast amounts of empty *space*.[40]

The primary quality of space is unchanging, imperturbable *presence*. It's always there, surrounding and permeating everything, while remaining completely unaffected by whatever happens.

This unchanging presence is the Divine Masculine

Presence is what the Feminine finds irresistibly attractive. She literally craves to be penetrated and pervaded by a man's presence and to know that no matter what she or life throws at him, he won't run, recoil or otherwise collapse.[41]

The primary quality of stuff is *radiant life force*. Whether it's light, energy or matter, stuff is visible and in constant motion, always changing, dancing, moving and flowing. With stuff, something is *always* happening. And in accordance with Newton's law that says, "for every action there's an equal and opposite reaction," stuff is affected by, and responds to, everything it comes in contact with.

This radiant life force is the Divine Feminine

---

[39] Jesus was called both "Son of God" (spirit) and "Son of Man" (flesh).

[40] Those of you who are familiar with non-duality teachings will take exception to me separating the One Life into two. Even though duality is an illusion, it's useful for our purposes here.

[41] Not all men have a Masculine essence and not all women have a Feminine one, something I'll point out later in this chapter. Also, I realize not every relationship is the traditional, heterosexual kind and this teaching applies to homosexual relationships as well. But for communication purposes, I'll speak as if the reader is heterosexual, with the man being Masculine and the woman being Feminine. Make adjustments for yourself as necessary.

Radiant life force is what the Masculine finds irresistibly attractive. He literally wants her to "light up his life," and to respond to his penetrating presence.

This is the divine *intercourse* of the Masculine and Feminine: *She craves His uncollapsible, trustable presence to contain her energy and penetrate her heart with love, while He, in turn, craves Her radiant life force to inspire His purpose, rejuvenate His being and to fully respond to His presence.*

When a man learns how to give his Masculine gift of presence, and when a woman learns how to give her Feminine gift of radiance, they will NEVER be single for long.

Are you interested in learning how to do this?

8 Distinctions

Before we fully explore Masculine/Feminine dynamics and how to use these energies to attract lasting love, it's important to make 8 very important distinctions:

1. *Polarity Chemistry is not love, nor is it romance.* It is the magnetic arc of energy that flows between the Masculine and Feminine poles. Love, on the other hand, is a wide-open heart and has nothing to do, necessarily, with sexual attraction. You can love your partner, of course, but you can also love a parent, a child, a book, a sport or a car. You don't need Polarity Chemistry for love, but you do need it for ongoing sexual attraction. Romance, or the feeling of falling in love, is also very different from Polarity Chemistry. As we've seen, it's actually Persona Chemistry, where one person's childhood wounding matches another's.

2. *Masculine and Feminine does not mean "man" and "woman."* They are universal energies that exist everywhere and within every human being. We all have both energies, though the vast majority of us identify with one more than the other. (It's like being right-handed or left-handed. We have both hands, but we naturally prefer one over the other.)

3. *The vast majority of men identify with Masculine energy and the vast majority of women identify with Feminine energy—but not all.* Some women, like Hillary Clinton, have a Masculine essence,

while some men, like Steven Tyler, lead singer for *Aerosmith*, have a Feminine essence. (That's how those two appear to me. I don't know either of them.)

4. *Masculine and Feminine energy exists on a continuum.* People can be extremely or moderately Masculine or Feminine, and a small percentage of people are 50/50, feeling equal preference for, say, a bloody boxing match or a chick flick.

5. *Energetic polarity is the attraction factor in any relationship—gay or straight.* If sexual attraction exists, two people, no matter their gender or sexual orientation, are animating opposite energies. (Ellen DeGeneres and Portia de Rossi, both women, are attracted to one another because Ellen has Masculine energy and Portia has Feminine energy. Again, this is my judgment from a distance.)

6. *Masculine and Feminine energies carry equal value.* Even though we live in a culture that still values the Masculine over the Feminine, neither is better or worse than the other. Additionally, both have a "dark" side and can be used in service of love or ego.

7. *True maturity is being able to access either energy according to the need of the moment.* Whether your dominant energy is Masculine or Feminine, a mature person can access their Masculine energy when direction is needed or they can access their Feminine energy when nurture is needed.

8. *The key to healthy attraction is to magnify your sexual energy in relational settings.* In other words, even though you have both energies and can access either when needed, THE GOAL IS NOT TO BE BALANCED, but to magnify your dominant sexual essence when you're around potential partners.

Now that we've defined Masculine and Feminine and made these distinctions, we are ready to take a closer look at "space and stuff" and better understand their radically different priorities, patterns and passions.

Attraction Factors

1. Are you a New York person or a Hawaii person? Are you more concerned with your direction toward freedom (Masculine) or the flow of love in your life (Feminine)?

2. Record your reflections on the Divine Masculine being described as *Presence* and the divine *Feminine* being described as Radiance. What do those words mean to you?

21

The Masculine/Feminine Dance

"Sexual Fulfillment in intimacy is not based on neutrality, but on the attractive differences, playful opposition and pleasurable nonequivalence of the Masculine and Feminine gifts, anatomical, emotional and spiritual."

~ David Deida

Having defined Masculine and Feminine energy as "Space and Stuff," and made some qualifying distinctions as to how they're to be understood, we're ready to go deeper. Let's take a look at how these two divine energies "dance" with one another by comparing and contrasting their styles.

Comparing the Masculine and Feminine

Item	Masculine	Feminine
Essence...	Imperturbable Presence	Radiant Life Force
Passion...	Search for Freedom	Search for Love
Priority...	Compete at the Edge of Death	Connect to the Depth of Life
Manner...	Focus and Finish	Flow and Feel
Under Stress...	Retreat to the Man Cave	Engage in Giri Talk
Addictions...	Numb Out, Emptiness	Feel Alive, Fullness
Gets Lost In...	Thoughts, Projects, Goals	Feelings, People, Drama
Primary Gift...	Directionality in Chaos	Rejuvenation from Stress

Essence...

One of the best ways to understand the Masculine/Feminine dance is by comparing them to the two major parts of a river: The banks and the water (space and stuff). The banks represent Masculine **imperturbable presence**. They contain, hold and guide the water. The water represents the Feminine. Without banks, the water goes everywhere. You could say it becomes a "hot mess." Likewise, without water, the banks are nothing more than a dry, empty hole in the ground.

The Feminine desires to be contained and guided by deep Masculine presence. She longs to relax and flow freely within its loving, directional embrace. The Masculine desires to be filled by the **radiant life force** of the wild and sensual Feminine. Its flow and wetness enliven its otherwise empty, dry existence.

Passion...

The Masculine passion, or preoccupation, is the **search for freedom**. It's the driving force behind everything it does. To a Masculine person, life often feels constraining, whether it's financial, spiritual, physical or relational, and so his deepest passion is to be free of any and all constraint.

This explains why the Masculine generally resists commitment and marriage. He perceives it as inhibiting his freedom, not enhancing it. However, when the Masculine feels that a woman's radiant life force supports his search for freedom and actually makes him more likely to achieve his chosen mission, he will joyfully devote himself to her. *The woman who knows how to support and enhance a man's search for freedom through her radiant life force is never single for long.*

Understanding that the Masculine search is for freedom and the Feminine search is for love explains why single men, in principle, are happier than single women. For a man, being single doesn't keep him from experiencing his heart's desire, which is freedom, but for a woman, it does, because her heart's desire is love.[42] Therefore, it's more difficult for a woman to be single *and* radiant than it is for a man to be single *and* present. Her radiance is affected by the degree to which love is flowing, or not flowing in her life, but the strength of his presence is not. That's affected by how deeply he's aligned with his purpose, which has nothing to do with the quality of his love life.

---

[42] I'm speaking of intimate love in this context. There are at least 5 other kinds of love a woman can experience that do not require an intimate partner and she should cultivate them in her life so that her happiness is not determined by her relationship status. For a thorough discussion of the six kinds of love, see chapter 8 in my first book, *Relationship Addiction—A Memoir*.

The Feminine passion, or preoccupation, is the **search for love**. It's the driving force behind everything she does. No matter how successful or powerful a Feminine person may be in her professional life, her deepest pleasure, and her deepest pain, comes from how much, or how little, love is flowing in her life. *The man who knows how to support and enhance a woman's search for love through his imperturbable presence is never single for long.*

Priority...

Nothing makes the Masculine feel more alive than **competing** (against himself or others) when something significant is at stake. He loves to test his limits and abilities in the office or on the golf course, and the closer he is to the edge of "death"—risking it all on a business venture or needing a putt on the last hole to beat his buddy—the more alive he feels. If a man can't compete for whatever reason (or even if he can), he gets almost as much joy out of watching others compete, thus the popularity of the *NFL*.

Conversely, nothing makes the Feminine feel more alive than when she's able to **connect** with others in deeply personal ways. Heaven to the Feminine is when matters of the heart are being authentically explored and expressed. It gives her as much joy as a touchdown does to the Masculine. If a woman can't connect deeply with others for whatever reason (or even if she can), she gets almost as much joy out of watching others connect, thus the popularity of shows like *The Bachelor*.

Manner...

The Masculine's manner is to block out all distraction, put his entire attention on one thing and complete it. In other words, his M.O. is to **focus and finish**. The Masculine is terrible at multi-tasking and hates being interrupted when it's working on a project, be it writing a book or watching a ballgame. His manner is clarity, direction, structure and self-discipline.

The Feminine, on the other hand, is a genius at multi-tasking. She can do many things at once—chatting with a friend, while sending a work email, while making dinner—but because she **flows and feels** her way through life, she doesn't mind being interrupted and she will drop what she's doing to help someone she cares about. Her manner is sensitivity, responsiveness, intuition and support.

138

Under Stress...

The Masculine experiences stress when it feels constrained, trapped or burdened by the demands of world, work and women. Because he's "space" and empty-ness, he will **retreat to the man cave** to reestablish his emotional equilibrium. In the man cave, which might be the golf course, the gym, a sports bar, an actual room, or, in my case, a cemetery, he'll attempt to reconnect to his deepest purpose and come up with a new plan of action. In other words, the Masculine goes into isolation to deal with stress.

The Feminine experiences stress when she feels a lack of loving connection in her life. Because she's "stuff" and something-ness, she will not go into isolation, but will seek community, connection and conversation when stressed. It's in these moments that the single woman desires and misses the Masculine's imperturbable presence the most. If he's not present (and even if he is), she'll **engage in girl-talk** to help find her emotional equilibrium.

Addictions...

All addictions are an attempt to medicate emotional pain. The Masculine pain is either feeling like his chosen mission is failing or when he feels constrained by responsibility. The Feminine pain is feeling a lack of deep, loving connection with a man and/or with anyone else she cares about. Therefore, even though men and women can be addicted to the same substances or activities, they use them for very different reasons.

When a Masculine person feels overwhelmed, burdened and pressured by some aspect of life, he turns to substances and activities to **numb-out** those feelings and be free of them. (This is, of course, pseudo-freedom.) Life has trapped him and he wants out, so he turns to things like alcohol, drugs, porn, gambling or TV. The "meds" are used to escape his pain.

When a Feminine person feels empty, lonely, abandoned or unloved, she turns to substances and activities that make her **feel alive**, full, loved and connected. (This, too, is pseudo-love.) Love is not flowing and filling her heart and body so she turns to food (usually chocolate, it's the Feminine equivalent to "porn") alcohol, romance novels or shopping to feel alive and filled with love.

If we learned to give each other our native gifts in intimacy, our need for "medication" would largely dissolve.

Gets Lost In...

Since the core of the Masculine is directionality and achieving its chosen mission, it often gets lost in, or consumed by, **thoughts, projects and goals**. In other words, a person with Masculine energy gets stuck in his head, obsessing about his purpose and his plans to achieve it.

For example, my current mission is to get this book out into the world. It's not uncommon for me to sit down at my desk at 6:00am, begin writing, and go all day without eating, dressing or showering. It just never occurs to me. I can get so lost in my head that I basically forget that I even have a body!

The Masculine, left to itself, is a very unbalanced, and potentially unhealthy energy. Its obsessive commitment to a transcendent vision and calling can cause the Masculine to lose contact, not only with its own body, but with beauty, nature, people and feelings. Basically, he loses contact with life!

The same thing happens to the Feminine, but in reverse. Since the core of the Feminine is the flow of love in relationship, she gets lost in **feelings, people and drama**. As the Masculine obsesses about plans and results, so the Feminine obsesses about people and relationships. The Feminine, also, when left to itself, is a very unbalanced and potentially unhealthy energy. It gets enmeshed in other people's problems and even overwhelmed by her own emotions. She often feels like a ship caught in a storm without a compass and a rudder, driven and tossed by emotional waves and unable to find her way.

Primary Gift... (Masculine)

Like a ship's compass and rudder or a river's banks, the Masculine gift is guidance and **directionality in chaos**. The Masculine, which can be thought of as divine GPS, knows where it is, where it wants to be and what it needs to do to get there.

Nothing gives the Masculine more joy than when his gift is requested, received and respected (i.e., followed). A man comes to life when he senses or sees some sort of chaotic or confusing situation and he's able to provide both a perspective and a plan to solve the problem. That's erotic to the Masculine.

This is why Masculine men are not sexually attracted to self-sufficient women.[43] Why would a man who wants to express his love through direction and guidance, be attracted to a woman who already knows where she wants to go and how she's going to get there? What's the point? She doesn't want or need his primary gift. A Masculine man is always looking for a wet, flowing woman who needs his "river banks," someone who's willing to receive emotional, spiritual, sexual or financial guidance.

When I met my wife, she was a highly functioning single woman with a master's degree and a good job. She was no "damsel in distress." But from the moment we first met (described in the Prologue), I felt her open to my guidance, emotionally and spiritually. And she still does. It was a turn on then, it's a turn on now. It's why I'm still attracted to her.

Not long ago, there was some drama going on in my wife's family and it was really bothering her. I resisted my initial instinct, which was to fix her. Instead, I was simply present, listening and being with her as she expressed her feelings. After a while though, it became clear that she was stuck, and her darkening mood was closing her heart more and more. I began sensing that what she needed was to take a long walk in the hot, summer Florida sun with me and I suggested that to her.

At first she stubbornly resisted my "directionality in chaos." In fact, she outright refused. But I persisted, remaining imperturbable in my presence, and she finally, but reluctantly, agreed to my plan. Not 15 minutes into our walk she looked at me and said that the walk was exactly what she needed. She felt emotionally free and relaxed. I could see it in her face. The light had returned to her eyes.

I, of course, took full, fun advantage of this moment, making her admit I was right. It was hilarious. I made her say, out loud, hands outstretched to the heavens, "Roy was right. He knows what I need better than I do." I teased her further, "Oh, come on. Say it like you mean it!" She could barely choke the words out, but I could tell how deeply she loved me in that moment. I had used my Masculine gift to free her from emotional chaos. I opened her heart and more importantly, she let me. (That's an important point. In this "dance," she let me lead. Ladies, are you willing to do such a thing?)

Finally, notice that even though the Masculine and Feminine energies are polar opposites, the little crossing arrows point to how beautifully they

---

[43] If this sentence triggers you, keep reading. I'm not arguing that a woman be a "damsel in distress," only that she not "wear the pants" in relationship settings. This will be explained further in this chapter and the ones that follow."

complement each other. The Masculine gift is perfectly suited to serve the Feminine in the area where she gets lost, and vice versa, as you're about to see.

Primary Gift... (Feminine)

The primary gift of the Feminine is the **rejuvenation from stress.** This too, beautifully complements the deepest Masculine need, which is relief from the stress of his mission. Hawaii-like Feminine energy is just what the New York guy needs. Her intuition and deep sensitivity make her a genius at knowing exactly how and when the Masculine needs to unplug and re-connect with his heart and hers.

Each day as I work on this book, I look forward to what my wife has planned for me in the evening. That time of day is hers. She organizes something that she feels I/we need to reconnect with each other or some-thing that will simply rejuvenate me. It may be something involving her body and mine; it may be going out to dinner, or staying in, watching a movie and eating something delicious she's prepared.

No matter what it is, I rarely go against her Feminine intuition. That's her domain. She knows about recovery. In fact, just the other day, she sug-gested we take a short vacation in a couple of months, which is when I'm projected to finish this book. I never think about vacations. They're a waste of time to me. But that's not healthy, so her Feminine gift balances me and protects me from myself.

As I've said, the Feminine is radiant life force, or better put, *a radiant force for life.* She stands for the heart rather than the head, for sensuality rather than success, for nature rather than numbers, for play rather than plans. Her greatest joy is to notice stress, suffering or even seriousness, and then to encourage, entice and enchant the Masculine away from his projects and into her world, not out of lonely selfishness, but to restore and rejuve-nate his soul.

This Feminine force is not always expressed quietly and gently, how-ever. In fact, what the Masculine often needs is her wrath as much as her warmth, her sword as much as her sweetness, her challenge as much as her caress. The ultimate allegiance of the Feminine is to Love (not men, or even herself), and she will stand for it and enforce it, by any means necessary.

Conclusion

Now that we've turned away from Persona Chemistry and learned about Polarity Chemistry, we're ready to fully express our authentic Masculine or Feminine essences and use that energy to attract lasting love.

When a man is divinely Masculine, I call him a *Superior Man*. When a woman is divinely Feminine, I call her a *Radiant Woman*.

In the following chapters, we'll look at each of them and also discuss some practical ways we can magnify these energies in our lives.

We'll begin with a close look at Radiant Women and then we'll look at Superior Men, but guys, don't skip the chapters on the divine Feminine. The same goes for the ladies. Be sure to read the chapters on the divine Masculine. *Mastering Masculine/Feminine dynamics means we must intimately understand both energies, not just our own.*

Attraction Factors

1. What insights or reflections do you take away from the side-by-side comparison of the Masculine and Feminine energies?

2. How will you act differently in the dating scene now that you see the different priorities and passions of each energy?

3. Ladies, describe three practical ways you could support a man's search for freedom.

4. Men, describe three practical ways you could support a woman's search for love.

22

Defining Feminine Radiance

*"Something in the way she moves, attracts me like no other lover;
Something in the way she woos me, I don't want to leave her now..."*

~ The Beatles

What is that *"something"* that *The Beatles* sing about so beautifully?[44] What is it about a woman that not only sparks initial attraction, but evokes a man's full devotion, to the point that he would say, "I don't want to leave her now"? Is it just a meaningless, romantic love song, or does it reflect something deeper? *Is there something that makes a woman irresistible to a man?*

Absolutely. That *something* is what I call Radiance. [45]

When a man meets a radiant woman, someone who "lights up his life," he not only wants her sexually, but he claims her heart completely and devotes himself to her eternally.

Call me psychic, but I think you're interested in that.

So we begin by defining what radiance is, and frankly, what it isn't. There are some important issues that surface when we discuss Feminine radiance, so this chapter is devoted to clarifying what radiance is NOT, and the next chapter is all about what radiance is.

What Radiance Does *NOT* Mean

The discussion of radiant women and present men is very important because when we don't fully embody our native sexual essence, be it Masculine or Feminine, it forms the sixth barrier to attracting lasting love. Dull women don't attract Present men and distracted men don't attract Radiant

---

[44] Enjoy. http://bit.ly/1l4zfEg

[45] For an even deeper discussion of this subject, see my video-based eCourse, The Radiant Woman: Evoking a Man's Full Devotion.

women. So I'm going to challenge us all to fully step into our divine callings.

But I'm very concerned about being misunderstood, especially by women. This discussion should be a joyful and playful exploration of your deepest nature, ladies, but if I'm misunderstood, you could feel discouraged or even depressed, so I want to point out 4 things that radiance does NOT mean.

1. *Radiance does NOT mean physical, conventional beauty.* It has nothing to do with having pouty lips, flawless skin, high cheekbones or big breasts. It's not about your age, your dress size or whether or not you wear designer label clothing. In other words, radiance is not reserved for *Victoria's Secret* models. (Personally, I think Queen Latifah is one of the most radiant women in Hollywood and she certainly doesn't have a runway model's appearance.) However, even though radiance is not about physical beauty, it is about energetic beauty, and that can be physically seen. It's "something in the way she *moves.*" So, I define radiance this way:

Radiance is the degree to which a woman allows love and light to flow freely through her Feminine form

Poet Maya Angelou calls this kind of woman a *Phenomenal Woman.*[46] Notice how she speaks about *the way she moves* rather than her appearance:

> *I walk into a room*
> *Just as cool as you please,*
> *And to a man,*
> *The fellows stand or*
> *Fall down on their knees.*
> *Then they swarm around me,*
> *A hive of honey bees.*
> *I say,*
> *It's the fire in my eyes,*
> *And the flash of my teeth,*
> *The swing in my waist,*
> *And the joy in my feet.*
> *I'm a woman*
> *Phenomenally.*

---

[46] Here is Maya Angelou reciting the entire poem: http://bit.ly/1k2IfLw

2. *Radiance does NOT mean uniformity or conformity.* In other words, not all phenomenal, radiant women are the same, nor should they be. Each radiant woman will have her unique way of expressing the divine Feminine. In a way, radiant women are like a strand of multi-colored Christmas lights. Each bulb has the same light within, but since the casings are shaded in different colors, each bulb shines differently. Therefore, no two radiant women are alike.

3. *Radiance does NOT mean every man will want you.* First of all, men who lack presence are scared to death of radiant women because radiant women won't put up with their mediocrity or bullshit. But even really good men will not always be attracted to every radiant woman because they have their particular tastes and preferences (as do women). The point of this teaching is that the divine Feminine always attracts the divine Masculine, and vice versa, but personal preferences do play a part.

4. *Radiance does NOT mean morphing into a man's image.* This is not about what men want; it's about who you already are. The idea being presented here is not "focus-grouping" men to see what they want and then packaging, positioning and promoting yourself as that. Chameleon-like neediness is actually the complete opposite of how a truly radiant woman moves. Her commitment is to discover and display her authentic, radiant self, and if that unique expression doesn't work for some guy, or anybody else for that matter, well, that's just too bad. A radiant woman stands in her own power and says, "Here I am. Are you strong enough to be my man?" Now, it just so happens that really good men find this sort of confidence sexy in women. But morphing into some man's image is not what we're talking about.

Attraction Factors
1. Four things were mentioned that radiance is NOT. Which one(s) speak to you the most and why?

2. When you compare conventional beauty with Maya Angelou's version, what differences stand out to you?

3. Describe a situation where you morphed into a man's image and became a chameleon to get him to want you.

— 23 —

The Irresistibly Radiant Woman

"What does he find spiritually sexy in you? He is irresistibly drawn into the light of your love, showing through your entire body as radiant openness and devotional surrender. The openness of this love-light is what your man finds spiritually sexy."

~ David Deida

In the last chapter, I defined radiance as the degree to which a woman allows Love's light to flow freely through her Feminine form. In that sense, a radiant woman is just like a precious diamond, which is also judged by how it reflects light. Of a diamond's "4C's"—Carat, Cut, Color and Clarity—it's the diamond's Cut that makes it sparkle and determines it's overall beauty.

Similarly, there are 6 facets of the divine Feminine, and they too, make a woman sparkle. When a woman is "cut" in these 6 ways, she becomes an irresistibly radiant woman. Let's take a look at them one at a time.[47]

Facet #1: She Expresses her Life Force—*Playfully*

When relationship experts teach on topics like attraction, dating and intimacy, we can make it sound pretty complicated. You might get the impression that you need to be a relationship rocket scientist in order to get a damn date! Now, while I do believe the best treasure is found in the deepest water, when it's all said and done, attracting lasting love may be as simple as this:

How much fun are you to be around?

---

[47] It's quite possible that you may feel overwhelmed by these 6 facets. Frankly, I haven't seen many women able to grow in all these areas without direct, one-on-one support. I'm a coach and helping women evolve in these ways is my specialty. Please reach out to me for support if you want to more fully embody these qualities in your life. My contact info is on the last page of the book.

No matter how conventionally beautiful a woman is, how long will anyone date "Debbie Downer?"[48] We all want someone to love us, but it's more important that someone like us.

So, how fun are you to be around? Are you a playful woman who's light-hearted, able to flirt, tease, laugh and have a good time, especially at your own expense? Or are you a serious, somber sour-puss and a drag to be around? As *Ferris Bueller* said of his friend: "Cameron is so tight that if you stuck a lump of coal up his ass, in two weeks you'd have a diamond."[49] Do you have a "Cameron" persona? Are you boring, tight and serious? Let me ask it this way: *Would you want to date you?*

The Feminine is radiant life force and when that flows freely through the Feminine form, it shines—*playfully*. Of course, the Feminine can be tenderhearted or even serious when appropriate, but normally she's playful, happy to be alive and fun to be around. This doesn't mean that every woman is supposed to be an extroverted "Chatty-Cathy" type, but it does mean, as Maya Angelou put it, that there's, "...*the swing in my waist, and the joy in my feet."* A phenomenal woman is a playful woman.

My clients often complain that their friends are "guy magnets" and they aren't. It's almost always because their friend is way more fun than they are. So, how playful are you? How much fun are you to be around? This is the first facet of the divine Feminine. Radiant women are playful women.

Facet #2: She Emanates her Sensuality—*Bodily*

Picture this: Two beautiful women are walking down the street side by side. It's a gorgeous, sunny day, and they're going to the same place for the same reason. Furthermore, they're dressed exactly alike, which is fitting because they're identical twins. Can you picture that? Everything is the same, except...

The first woman's body is really stiff, controlled and tight. Her chin is set, her lips are pursed, her breath is shallow, her eyes are locked on target, her hips are rigid, her walk is purposeful and her mind is focused. She's on a mission to get to where she's going.

The second woman's body is quite different. She's flowing, almost sashaying down the street, alive with energy and motion. She moves more like a runway model than her drill sergeant twin sister. Her hips swing

---

[48] This goes for men too. No one wants to date "Danny Downer" either.

[49] Enjoy. http://bit.ly/1ijT6MT

rhythmically to a silent song and her eyes joyfully land, linger and leap from face to face. Every so often she stops to soak in the sun's rays, quietly moaning in delight at the warmth on her face. She seems to be making love to the moment, breathing every sight, smell and sound into her body, and with a smile and an occasional sassy wink, she exhales her love to the world through her heart.

Which one of these women would you be more attracted to?

A radiant woman is a sensual, flowing, body-oriented creature. Of course she can make plans and decisions and use her head when necessary, but she prefers the sensual realm of emotion, pleasure and sensation. Whether it's digging around in the dirt or feeling fabrics against her skin or swooning from the scent of her favorite coffee or being pleasured by a man for hours, life is experienced in her body. She wants to feel rather than think, dance rather than decide and smell rather than strategize, though she can do either when needed.

The more a woman allows herself to live sensually from below her neck, the more alive and happy she'll feel. And when a woman feels happy to be alive, she beams like the sun. So, if you want to attract your ideal man, you must give yourself permission to be sensual and even cultivate sensuality in your life.

So, of the twins described, which one are you most like, in general? Are you more like the stiff girl or the sensual one? If I saw you walking in a grocery store, would you be focused on your list, purposefully getting things done and keeping to your schedule? Or, would you be alive with love, flowing sensually through the store, having "intercourse" with everything from produce to people—as you got things done? In other words, in normal, everyday situations like grocery shopping, are you in your head or are you in your body? Are you in your Masculine or your Feminine?

Remember, it's during these normal moments that you're going to meet someone. My wife met me at a conference, for example. She was getting CE credits for work. She had no thought of meeting a man. She was just living life. But, if you read the Prologue, you saw how playful she was with me and she felt very sensual to me too, all of which made her irresistible.

Facet #3: She Exposes her Heart—*Vulnerably*

The third facet of the divine Feminine is, perhaps, the most challenging one of all. The first two, being playful and sensual, may not be easy, but at least they're enjoyable! Being vulnerable, however, is not something any sane person would call "fun." Nevertheless, a radiant woman recognizes

150

that it's her divine calling to live as Love's light whether it's pleasurable or not. And so as scary as it might be, and as often as she's been hurt, a radiant woman refuses to close her heart and protect herself from pain. She, instead, makes the moment-to-moment *frightening* choice to live with an open heart and take the risk of being hurt.

> **Nothing is sexier to a man than an emotionally undefended, "naked," vulnerable woman.**

Good men find it incredibly erotic to meet a woman whose arms are not crossed (metaphorically speaking), but are, instead, spread wide open, revealing a deep yearning to be embraced and claimed. However, such a "posture" is scary for many women. To be vulnerable, real and utterly raw in the presence of a man is terrifying. And many women refuse. For them, the risk is just too great. And while I honor such feelings and understand them, they have negative consequences.

A couple of chapters back, I made a provocative statement that men aren't sexually attracted to self-sufficient women. Here's why: Far too often, what lies behind the self-sufficient, independent woman is a hardened, defended, impenetrable heart. She's been hurt and she'll never allow herself to be hurt again. That's understandable, but unfortunately, good men can feel those walls of closure and resistance, and they'll stay away.

Now, I am NOT saying a radiant woman is one who embraces any man with a pulse or has sex with the first guy who says, "Hello." That's not a radiant woman; that's an insecure one. Let me say this clearly: A radiant woman has firm boundaries and she willingly enforces them (see Facet 4). She does not put up with frat-boys, bad-boys, mama's boys, phony boys or phobic boys. In fact, she only opens *completely* in the presence of a deeply trustable man. But a radiant woman's normal, everyday "posture" is to have an open, yearning, undefended heart, refusing to play games or protect herself from the possibility of pain.

What is the condition of your heart in this moment? Is it vulnerable or is it protected? Keep this in mind: Safe hearts are single hearts.

Facet #4: She Enforces her Love—*Fiercely*

The danger in our discussion of the divine Feminine so far is that you might have the impression that a radiant woman is a soft, sweet, sincere "flower" who wouldn't hurt a fly. Nothing could be further from the truth.

A radiant woman is all that, but she also wields a very sharp sword and she will use it in the service of Love.

The Hindu goddess, Kali, best represents this fierce facet of the divine Feminine. "Kali is the fearful and ferocious form of the mother goddess...Kali is represented with perhaps the fiercest features amongst all the world's deities. She has four arms, with a sword in one hand and the head of a demon in another."[50] The message is clear: You don't mess with a radiant woman. When you're in her presence, you better be aligned with love and truth or you'll face her wrath.

The fourth facet of the divine Feminine is about anger, and while a whole book could be written on this subject, my purpose here is only to help you see that anger is a positive emotion (when used properly) and that a radiant woman uses it to enforce Love. But unfortunately, many women have disowned their anger, feeling that it's a negative emotion and that it has no place in relationships. That's understandable, since so many women have seen first hand how destructive anger can be, but it's also tragic. Anger is simply an energy that says, "NO!" and it's extremely important for a woman to be able to say that little word.

This facet balances the previous one. A radiant woman's anger ensures that her vulnerability isn't abused or mistaken for weakness. Yes, her arms are wide open, but like Kali, she has a sword in one of them! In this sense a radiant woman is like Jesus, who was both "gentle and humble at heart" and someone who would go into a rage to enforce a boundary.[51]

When it comes to relationships, non-radiant women get angry when they don't get what they want. Their sword is used selfishly. A radiant woman's sword, however, is used sacredly. Her anger is not used to get what she wants, but for what Love wants. A radiant woman's anger is kindled when she witnesses men falling short of their divine calling and capability. It angers her when she sees men mired in mediocrity, cruelty, insensitivity or inauthenticity. She challenges such men, not to get what she wants, but to see them be the men she knows they're capable of being.

Facet #5: She Expresses her Truth—*Spontaneously*

In the 1992 movie, *A League of Their Own,* Tom Hanks manages a all-girls baseball team. Perhaps its most famous scene is the one where Hanks berates one of the girls for a bad play and she begins to cry, to which he

---

[50] http://abt.cm/1rmm9Tm
[51] Matthew 11:28-30 and John 2:14-16

152

screams, "There's no crying in baseball!"[52] In other words, baseball is not a place for emotional expression, especially sadness. That's "girl stuff" and it doesn't belong.

Now, I recognize it's just a movie, but that's a message our Masculine dominated culture has given women for centuries. "Girl stuff"—emotional expression—is not welcome. There's a general dislike, perhaps even disdain for the Feminine way. Consequently, most women are afraid of expressing their true feelings, especially around men, who far too often run, recoil or even retaliate when they do. So women have learned to hide their emotions, or at least be very careful in how they express them.

The radiant woman refuses to do this. She is life force and she isn't embarrassed or apologetic about her emotional way. She will not hide her feelings because of societal pressure or men's incapacity. She's committed to expressing her truth—*spontaneously*. In other words, a radiant woman's emotional expression is raw, real and *right away.*[53]

The best way to understand the art of spontaneous expression is to think about how you have sex. For example, when a man touches you in a way that feels really good, do you tell him the next day, or a week later, how good that felt, or does your body spontaneously moan or scream, "Oh God, YES!"? The answer is obvious. You respond without *hesitation.* Likewise, if he's touching you in a way that hurts, you don't wait a few days to tell him, do you? You immediately say, "Ouch! Stop, that hurts!".

But not only do you respond without hesitation, you also respond without *restraint*, meaning, your sexual expression matches the amount of pleasure or pain felt in your body. If it feels a little good, you moan a little; when it feels incredible, you moan louder. Likewise, if it hurts a little, you say "ouch", if it hurts a lot, you throw him off the bed! In other words, your expression fully matches the feeling in your body.

The third way you have sex is without *thinking*, meaning, you're not in your head talking to yourself: "Should I tell him that hurts? What if he gets mad at me or thinks I'm too sensitive? I'll wait until it's a good time to tell him how I feel." That's not how you have sex. Your body just reacts without thought or evaluation. During an orgasm, you're not up in your head thinking, "I better not scream and writhe too much. He might think I'm weird." No, you're totally in your body. You're not judging, analyzing, or considering. You're just coming.

---

[52] Here's the scene: http://bit.ly/1mZvdkF

[53] The same goes for superior men too.

Finally, you have sex without *words*. Yes, you may say things like, "That's good. Faster, right there," etc., but basically, you make sounds, don't you? (and sometimes animal sounds!) When he's going down on you and it feels incredible, you're not saying, "Wow, the nerve endings in my clitoris are really sensitive and when your tongue touches me there, messages are transmitted through my neurotransmitters, up through my spinal column into my Medulla Oblongata where I'm able to interpret what's happening as pleasurable." You don't say a bunch of words. You just make sounds. Even if you could find the words to describe your feelings, you wouldn't want to use them. And the guy doesn't need them anyway. A groan, growl or gasp will tell him all he needs to know.

So, in bed, you express your feelings and emotions without (1) Hesitation, (2) Restraint, (3) Thinking and (4) Words. Your expression is real, raw, reactive and right away. Here's the principle I'm getting at:

A radiant woman relates like she fucks

A radiant woman, whether she's in bed with a man or on a first date, unapologetically and spontaneously expresses her true feelings without hesitation, restraint, thinking or words. Let me be more specific.

(1) *Without Hesitation.* A radiant woman shares her feelings with a man as soon as she feels them. When he does something, it's immediately, "Yeah!" or "Yuck!" There's no hesitation. There is no space or time between action and reaction.

For example, let's say your date picks you up when he said he would, opens the car door for you and pulls out your chair at the table in the restaurant. When your glass of wine comes, you make a toast, saying, "Here's to a real gentleman. I can barely find the words to tell you what a turn on it is to be picked up on time and treated like a lady. I'm already looking forward to our second date."

However, during dinner, this same man is rude to the server. A radiant woman immediately says, "I did not like the way you treated our server. That really turned me off and it makes me wonder if you're the guy for me." Boom. *Real, raw and right away.*

(2) *Without Restraint.* A radiant woman does not worry about what a man will think or how he'll react to her true feelings. Therefore, she expresses them fully and authentically, without holding back. In other words, she's constantly reflecting how she's feeling her man, moment to moment.

154

Imagine a radiant woman being on a coffee date with a guy she met online and the date's going great. She really likes him and she's sort of wondering/hoping he'll ask her out again. As they're getting up to leave he says, "Hey, I've had a really nice time. Would you like to get together again?" Now, a non-radiant woman would say "yes," but she wouldn't let him know what she's really feeling for fear that it might scare him off or give him too much power. But a radiant woman expresses without restraint. She'd say, "Oh, God yes. In fact, I was just hoping you'd ask me out again because I really like you." Not only is she expressing her truth spontaneously, but she's also making herself vulnerable by exposing her true feelings.

(3) *Without Thinking.* Non-radiant women try to figure out what to say in order to control an outcome. They create mental stories and scenarios to help them decide whether or not to say anything. They're up in their heads calculating how something might be perceived and what results it's likely to produce. This is very exhausting and diminishes a woman's radiance.

A radiant woman, however, drops the strategic thinking and simply commits to authenticity and blurting, which take no effort or thought whatsoever. She just blurts it out, raw and real.

(4) *Without Words.* This one is a little tricky because there is a time to engage in normal, verbal communication. But frankly, talking is overrated and the vast majority of it is unnecessary. There's a principle in conscious relationships called, "The One Outbreath Communication."[54] It means that if anything really important needs to be said, it can be said in one breath. When we get into long discussions, we usually fall into story-telling and making very arguable statements. Even the Bible says as much: "When there are many words, transgression is unavoidable, but he who restrains his lips is wise."[55]

Additionally, the Feminine has a hard time putting her feelings into logical, coherent, sentences anyway. Have you noticed how hard it is to describe your emotions with words? When you're really mad, don't you just want to scream? Well, then...*scream*! Don't try to find words. Instead, communicate by making sounds that reflect how you're feeling. Frankly, a guy will understand you better anyway. When my wife goes on and on, I tend to zone out. But when she gives me, for example, a loud, deep in the chest groan, I get her, which is what she wants.

---

[54] I learned this, and many other principles in this book, from Dr.'s Gay and Kathlyn Hendricks.
[55] Proverbs 10:19

Now, if something needs explaining, fine. Use words. But try communicating with sounds more frequently. The next time you're on a date with a guy, when he does or says something you like, moan at him seductively. If he does something you hate, say "yuck!" or better yet, make a growling sound.

Not only are sounds completely unarguable and authentic ways of communicating, they're playful too. It will freak him out and in that sense you're fulfilling Facet 1. A good man will be fascinated by, and attracted to, a woman who expresses her truth— spontaneously.

Facet #6: She Energizes her Man—*Sexually*

Women love sex. In fact, contrary to popular opinion, women are more sexual than men. The Feminine's very nature is love, so her hunger and capacity for a sexual relationship far exceeds the Masculine's. When a woman is with a man she can deeply trust, her sexual power is unleashed.[56] The reason men often appear to be more sexual than women is because women rarely find men worthy of their complete devotional surrender (something we're going to fix when we talk about superior men). But if they do find a trustable man, look out. Their bodies can transmit far more sexual energy than a man's. Men can have one orgasm and we're usually done for a while; a woman can have multiple orgasms and she can go all night.

So, the sixth facet of the divine Feminine is NOT about being sexual. All women are sexual, no matter how radiant they are.[57] Radiance increases a woman's sexual attractiveness, but it doesn't increase her sexual drive. *This facet is about the purpose of a woman's sexuality.* It's about why she has sex, not how.

There are three ways women use their sexuality, which are to (1) Control, (2) Connect or (3) Commune.[58] As the graphic shows, these three ways indicate different levels of a woman's willingness to surrender in a relationship. The more she opens in deep devotional surrender (to a man she can completely trust), the more radiant she becomes. Allow me to briefly describe these three ways a woman uses her sexuality.

---

[56] This "unleashing" is relative, depending upon a woman's age, hormone levels, her overall health and other factors.

[57] This is true unless the woman has barrier inhibiting her natural sexuality.

[58] These apply to men too, and in the graph, the vertical line would change from Radiance to Presence.

(1) *Control.* The first way a woman's sexuality can be used is to control men so that she can get the love and attention she needs. This would be "Suzy the Slut." She uses her sexuality to alleviate loneliness and the fear of being unlovable. There is no shame in this, however. We all go through times in our lives when we feel insecure and needy.[59] But when a woman is motivated by such things, her radiance is quite dim, and of course, when she's controlling men with her body, she never ultimately gets the love she seeks.

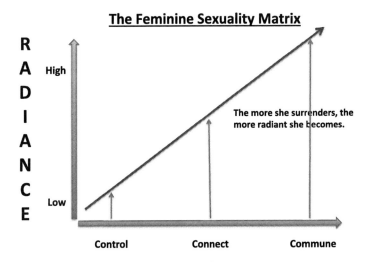

The Feminine Sexuality Matrix

R A D I A N C E

High

Low

The more she surrenders, the more radiant she becomes.

Control   Connect   Commune

S U R R E N D E R

(2) *Connect.* The second way a woman's sexuality can be used is to connect with a man. In the previous way, her selfishness created co-dependent, controlling relationships. Here, she's let go of her emotional neediness and is able to create a 50/50 style relationship, one of mutual respect, equal responsibilities and simultaneous orgasms. Because this is a much healthier motivation than the first, a woman's radiance shines much brighter. However, the emphasis on egalitarian balance indicates that a measure of fear is still operating. She's not allowing herself to be totally vulnerable. Therefore, even though a woman has made great progress moving from a controlling to a connecting motivation, her heart is still not fully surrendered to Love and her radiance will not shine as brightly as it could.

---

[59] I know I did. In fact, my first book is all about my move from stage 1 to stage 2.

(3) *Commune.* This is the stage at which a woman shines the brightest. Here, the radiant woman has surrendered, not to a man, but to Love itself. As David Deida says,

> "You long to surrender all control and allow love to move through your body and heart, so you can be utterly *possessed* by love. Your yearning to give yourself as love grows stronger than your need for a man to take care of you or for you to take care of yourself."

The purpose of a radiant woman's sexuality is way beyond selfishness or even mutual satisfaction. It's to commune with a man so deeply that both of them are energized to fulfill their destinies, hers as Love, his as Freedom. In other words,

The purpose of sex between a radiant woman and a superior man is to open each other to God.

When a man makes love to a radiant woman, he not only experiences the presence of God through the beauty of her open, sensual body, but his heart is energized to more passionately pursue his chosen purpose. In other words, to be with a radiant woman makes a man feel like he can conquer the world. In like fashion, when a woman makes love to a superior man, his depth of presence opens her heart and allows her to fully surrender to divine Presence. In other words, to be with a superior man makes a woman feel like she can embrace the world.

None of this has anything to do with sexual technique, by the way. Hell, both male and female porn stars are good in bed, but the men are not present and the women are not radiant, as I'm defining it here. They're simply "doing it" rather than spiritually dissolving together in two-bodied devotional surrender and trust.

Conclusion

These 6 facets of the divine Feminine are what make a woman shine like the sun. They are your birthright. It's who you are. It doesn't matter how old you are, how conventionally beautiful you are or what your dress size is. Though your radiance may be shrouded and covered over by fear, you are playful, sensual, vulnerable, fierce, spontaneous and sexual. *You are a radiant woman.*

The next two chapters are devoted to exploring the divine Feminine and I'm going to show you 4 ways you can block your radiance and then 4 ways you can brighten your radiance.

Attraction Factors

1. On a scale of 1-10, how fun are you to be around? What keeps you from being more playful?

2. Touch, taste, hearing, sight and smell are the five senses. Describe a specific way you can experience each one of them this week.

3. On a scale of 1-10, how vulnerable do you consider yourself to be? What keeps you from being more vulnerable?

4. Write an example of what it would look like in your life to express fierce anger in the service of Love.

5. On a scale of 1-10, how spontaneously do you express your feelings? What keeps you from being current with your thoughts and feelings?

6. There are three ways women use their sexuality: to control, connect or commune. Which one most characterizes your previous relationships? Give an example.

— 24 —

How to Raise Your Radiance, pt. 1

"...I'm a bitch, I'm a lover, I'm a child, I'm a mother
I'm a sinner, I'm a saint, I do not feel ashamed
I'm your hell, I'm your dream, I'm nothing in between
You know you wouldn't want it any other way.
So take me as I am
This may mean you'll have to be a stronger man
Rest assured that when I start to make you nervous
and I'm going to extremes
Tomorrow I will change and today won't mean a thing..."

~ *Bitch*
Meredith Brooks

Are you a bitch? If not, it's probably why you're still single.

Meredith Brooks' hit song, *Bitch*, is the best musical description of the divine Feminine I've ever heard and I would strongly encourage you to listen to its words closely.[60] Radiant women are bitches and the more superior a man is, the more he wants a radiant bitch.

Obviously, the word "bitch" is a derogatory and nasty term for women, and by now, I hope you can tell I have the utmost respect for you. I'm using the term playfully, just as Meredith Brooks is using it. We use it to describe the wild, unpredictable succulent nature of the divine Feminine. It's a term of endearment, not disrespect.

So in this chapter, I'm going to show you how to be a bigger bitch (smile) by pointing out 4 ways you can block your "bitch-ness." In the next chapter, I'll show you 4 ways to brighten your "bitch-ness."

The Feminine is High-Maintenance

What I love most about Meredith Brooks' song is that she owns that she's a high-maintenance pain in the ass. In one part of the song she says, "*I can understand how you'd be so confused, I don't envy you. I'm a little bit*

---

[60] Here's the whole song: http://bit.ly/11TFfv6

of everything all rolled into one." She knows what a challenge she is and she has compassion for what her man is faced with, moment-to-moment.

The fact of the matter is that most men can't handle radiant women. Their presence (space) isn't wide or deep enough to contain a woman's full emotional flow (stuff). As a result, men frequently pressure women to be less wild and emotional and more predictable and logical, in other words, more like them! You cannot allow yourself to be tamed or masculinized by weak, mediocre men. Own your high-maintenance-ness. Relish in your bitch-ness. It's beautiful and it's your essential nature. Don't be afraid of being "too much", instead, tell men, as Meredith does, "you'll have to be a stronger man."

Radiance Is Like the Sun

Before we get into the particular ways you can block and brighten your radiance, it's important that you understand that your "shine" is much like the sun's, in that both of you are always shining. Just as the sun is always shining, so you are too. When we can't see the sun's shine it's because we've either turned away from it (the earth has rotated) or there are clouds blocking its rays. It's the same way with your natural radiance. Love's light is always shining from your heart. You *are* a radiant woman. It's just that sometimes you've turned away from your radiance or you have "clouds" blocking its shine.

So your journey is not to *become* radiant. You *ARE* radiant. I quoted Michael Bernard Beckwith earlier, but it bears repeating:

> "Remember this: 100% of spiritual growth, development and unfoldment is about letting go of something; it's not about getting or acquiring something. It's about releasing something."

4 Bitch Blockers

There are 4 ways a woman can block her radiant "bitch-ness": Blaming, Believing, Business and Baggage. They are the things she must "release." Let's take a look at them one at a time.

Bitch Blocker #1: Blaming

Nothing dulls your shine more than being "Betty the Blamer." It's so easy to get caught in the darkening energy of the victim mentality, believing that life is hard, unfair and that you're being mistreated in some way. But finger pointing and believing that you're "right" (which makes others wrong, of course) diminishes your shine significantly. How playful, sensual and vulnerable can you be when your body is all knotted up with blame?

Take a moment of honest reflection: How much blaming, complaining, judging, whining, labeling, name-calling, arguing, gossiping, criticizing, guilt-tripping or shaming do you engage in regarding men, the dating scene, relationships and life in general?

Even though I'm going to show you 4 ways to brighten your shine in the next chapter, I want to give you a simple "radiance raising ritual" for each of the 4 Blocks. Think of them as antidotes to the disease that threatens your radiance.

Radiance Raising Ritual #1: *Gratitude.*

The simple practice of gratitude will raise your radiance and brighten your shine. It will open your heart and return the light to your eyes. But let's be careful not to confuse this deep sense of appreciation and thankfulness with circumstantial happiness. A radiant woman's gratitude is not rooted in the impermanent nature of life or even the degree to which human love is flowing in her life, but in a far deeper openness to the "is-ness" of the present moment. On gratitude, Eckhart Tolle has written,

> "It is a deep sense of Being-ness, or aliveness, and through that, you appreciate 'what is' in your life...You appreciate the many forms of life that are arising at this moment. You don't impose judgment on the form that life takes at this moment." [61]

Bitch Blocker #2: Believing

The second major issue that darkens a woman's natural radiance is when she believes the "voice in the head." Have you noticed the crazy shit that goes on between your ears? The voice criticizes you, tells stories about this or that, has imaginary arguments with others, invents scenarios of doom and so on. These thoughts and stories, *if they're believed*, will close your heart, shut you down and darken your radiance. For example...

- If you believe that all men are shallow assholes, how playful would you be around men?

---

[61] Here, Eckhart Tolle talks to Oprah on the topic of abundance and gratitude. It's a bit long, 10:00 minutes or so, but well worth the time. http://bit.ly/1sEloJd

- If you believe that all men are untrustworthy, how vulnerable would you allow yourself to be?
- If you believe that you're fundamentally unlovable, how spontaneously would you express your feelings and truth?
- If you believe that men only want "one thing," how sensual and sexual would you be?

What all this means is that if you *believe* that crazy voice in your head, if you take its stories to be true, you'll be an emotional mess, filled with anxiety, suspicion, anger and hopelessness. And that, girlfriend, is NOT attractive. The sparkle in your eyes, "the joy in your feet," and the radiance of your heart will all but disappear if you believe that your thoughts and stories are true.

Contrary to a lot of New Age baloney, you are not responsible for your thoughts, nor do you choose them. You have no control over what pops in your head. However, what you are responsible for, what you do choose, is whether or not you *attach* to those thoughts and believe that they're true.

The voice in the head has three themes:

(1) *There's something wrong with you.* The voice says, "I'm unlovable; I'm not good enough; I'm powerless; I'm stupid; I'm unwanted," etc., etc. These are called core stories of deficiency. We all have them.

(2) *There's something wrong with men.* The voice says, "Men are assholes; men are out for one thing; men want younger women; men don't commit," and so on.

(3) *There's something wrong with life.* The voice says, "All the good ones are taken or gay; I'm going to end up alone; online dating is filled with losers, liars and lunatics; no one wants a person with my life situation and baggage," etc.

There is not even a shred of truth in any of that. They're just made-up stories. In fact, in every one of those stories, the opposite could be as true or truer than the original story.[62] But when you believe the "voice in the head," your radiance will diminish.

Radiance Raising Ritual #2: *Inquiry*

The two best spiritual practices for ending our attachment to all three kinds of stories are *The Living Inquiries*, developed by Scott Kiloby[63] and

---

[62] "Story" is one of the 7 commitments in my *Dating Manifesto*, found in Appendix I.
[63] http://kiloby.com

The Work, developed by Byron Katie.[64] In the context of this book, all I can do is invite you to investigate these two amazing tools on your own.

Bitch Blocker #3: Business

One of the keys to attracting lasting love is to fully display your dominant sexual energy in relational settings. When a man's presence comes in contact with a woman's radiance, an arc of energy flows between them and they're attracted to each other. That's the whole point of this section of the book. It's what I've called, Polarity Chemistry. It's THE attraction factor.

Though we all have both energies, when we're around the opposite sex in relational settings, women must relax their Masculine sides and magnify their Feminine, and men must relax their Feminine sides and magnify their Masculine.

This is much harder for women to do than it is for men. Here's why: The workplace is, by definition, Masculine. It doesn't matter if you teach at an all-girls school, or work at *Victoria's Secret* or even if your entire company is made up of women, the workplace is Masculine. It's about goals, structure, direction, sales, budgets and getting the job done. That's all Masculine stuff.

When a woman works, then, she's not only entering a Masculine environment, *she's also animating her Masculine energy,* being asked to accomplish certain goals or complete specific tasks in a focused, timely manner. (The same is obviously true for men.)

Here's where it gets challenging. When a man leaves the professional realm and enters the relational realm, if he wants to attract the opposite sex, no shift in energy is required. He simply needs to continue expressing his present, purposeful Masculine energy like he has all day. No change is needed.

However, the woman has to make a huge shift at the end of her day. When she leaves the professional realm and enters the relational realm, she has to "disrobe," if you will, she has to deactivate the Masculine energy she's been running through her body all day, and reactivate her Femininity. If she doesn't, men will not feel sexual attraction toward her. They will respect her self-sufficient determination, but they won't feel the availability of her vulnerable heart, which is what a man finds irresistible.

This is why business is a major block to Feminine radiance:

---

[64] http://www.byronkatie.com

Running Masculine energy through a Feminine body all day dims Love's light and dulls your shine.

The answer to this dilemma is not, of course, for women to quit their jobs, nor should we go back to the strict gender roles of the 1950's. It's wonderful that women are giving their gifts to the world outside the home and enjoying much more economic freedom as a result. It's just that if women are going to be career-oriented, they have to do a little extra work to ensure they don't lose contact with their true Feminine heart and become masculinized women. That's done by committing to a Feminine spiritual practice I call *smudging*.

Radiance Raising Ritual #3: *Smudging*

Smudging is an ancient Native American ritual used to cleanse a person, place or an object of *negative* energies, spirits or influences.[65] Well, every career woman should smudge herself when she makes the transition from the professional to the personal realm. The Masculine energy that she's been running through her body all day should be treated as "*negative* energies, spirits and influences." Here are some practical smudging ideas, listed from the easiest to the most radical:

- Change your hair or makeup in some way before you leave work. In other words, alter your appearance to some degree, and the more, the merrier.
- If you're going out after work, bring a change of clothes. No matter how cute and Feminine your workday outfit is, do NOT go into the relational realm in the same clothes in which you worked. They've been contaminated.
- At the end of your day, when you leave your workplace, be it a cubicle, car, computer screen, building or office (even an office in your home), create a ceremony where you literally brush the Masculine energy off your body, as if you're trying to get lint off your clothing.
- Wiggle your body, swivel your head, shake your arms or maybe even twerk your hips. Wild, interpretive dancing would be ideal. The point is to release the rigid, structured energy from your body and reignite your Feminine flow. Also, make the motions big and dramatic. Get that "nasty" Masculine energy out of you.

---

[65] http://www.nativeamericanresearch.org/smudging.html

- Activate your playfulness by performing an exorcism on yourself. Again, before you leave your work space, say, "Come out of me, o' Masculine demon of direction and take possession of my body, o' Goddess of love and fill me with light." Sprinkle water on yourself if you have to. (Smile.)

This final one can be used when you leave your workplace, but it's best to do it before a date or before interacting with men in a relational setting.

- Create a breath/mantra ceremony where you intentionally deactivate your Masculine and reactivate your Feminine. It might look something like this: "I hereby deactivate my Masculine energy and leave it in this space and I activate my Feminine energy in my body and my heart." Then take a deep inhale and consciously imagine that as you exhale, you're pushing all of the Masculine energy out of your body. Wiggle and move as you do this. Empty your lungs until it almost hurts. Then, with a very slow, sensual inhale, consciously imagine breathing Feminine energy in through your nose and down into your body, filling your heart, breasts, belly and especially your vagina. Repeat until you sense all the Masculine is gone and the Feminine has filled every inch of your body. (I would not be surprised if you feel slightly aroused after doing this and that's a good thing. To be feeling sensual around men and slightly turned on is ideal.)

Bitch Blocker #4: Baggage

The fourth issue that blocks a woman's radiance is emotional baggage, and frankly, if you think about it, this entire book is about baggage. Each of the seven barriers is a kind of baggage, is it not? For example, personas are baggage (barrier #5), being incomplete with a former lover is baggage (barrier #4), being afraid of rejection or the loss of autonomy is baggage (barrier #3) and so on. So having pretty much identified every type of emotional baggage that can possibly sabotage our love lives, what more can be said about this subject?

Well, we haven't talked about the issue of trust. Nothing dulls and darkens a woman's shine more than having trust issues. Carrying past pain and hurt makes you apprehensive and suspicious at best, callous and closed, at worst.

It's literally impossible to display the 6 facets of the divine Feminine when you have trust issues.

Once in a while, I'll meet a woman who is self-aware enough to admit she has closed her heart completely to men and relationships because of past pain and hurt. That makes me sad, but at least she's aware of her choice and I honor that. More often, though, women are not aware of their trust issues. In fact, they often convince themselves that being a bit suspicious is wise and appropriate. Their posture is one of being closed *until* a man shows he can be trusted. Here's how it sounds:

> "My approach is to hold back and take a wait and see approach with men. Trust has to be earned. He has to prove himself and show me he's for real before I'll open my heart to him."

This perspective will keep you single.

Though it's an extremely common view, and one that, on the surface, seems to make sense, it's the signature statement of a person with huge trust issues. *It's also the exact opposite of being vulnerable.* A radiant, vulnerable woman's perspective is this:

> "My commitment is to meet every man with a vulnerable, wide open heart. I assume all men are good, honorable and trustworthy until they show me otherwise. The moment I sense a man is a loser or a liar, I'll chop off his balls and send him on his way."

The difference between those two perspectives is night and day. One begins with a closed heart, the other with an open heart. Why is this important? Because a good man can feel your suspicion and closure and it's a huge turn off. He's drawn to the light of your vulnerable, soft heart.

Picture a swimming pool and a slab of concrete. When a man puts his hand into the pool, the water receives and envelops his hand, taking its shape. A vulnerable heart feels like water. It receives him. But no good man wants to be forced to use a jackhammer to open your concrete heart.

Having that understanding, the question then is this: If men have hurt you, how do you trust them again? The answer: You don't.

A radiant woman never trusts men. In fact, she doesn't trust anything in this life. She realizes that everything is impermanent, and therefore, ultimately untrustworthy. Men come and go, feelings come and go, relationships come and go, people die, change their minds, do hurtful things and break their commitments. There is nothing solid and trustable in this life. Nothing.

A radiant woman's trust is not based upon the quality of a man, but on her intimate connection and trust in Life itself.

She trusts Love, God, Spirit, Oneness, the Absolute or whatever you call it. She does not trust fallible human beings. To do that would be to live in constant fear. But since her trust is in the spiritual rather than the relational realm, her heart can stay open, even if it's been hurt in the past, because what she trusts in never changes. She trusts that life is and always will unfold perfectly, and that whatever happens is a reflection of Perfection and ultimately for her good and growth.

A radiant woman's faith is not in a man's presence, but in the immovable, unchangeable, imperturbable Presence. This is why she lives without suspicion and closure and why she's open to every man she meets, even if her past has been filled with pain and betrayal.

Now, as we said earlier, a radiant woman is a discerning woman. She never ignores her intuition and she's no one's doormat. She fiercely enforces her boundaries, but she does so from an open, vulnerable heart. She trusts Love and Life, but she never trusts a guy—in the absolute sense.

Now, of course, the more superior a man is, the more she can relax and totally surrender in the relative trustworthiness of his love and presence. But ultimately, she has no idea what a man will do, who he really is and how a relationship will play out. And in the deepest sense, it doesn't matter. She knows her life is connected to something that never changes.

Do you see how viewing trust like this makes it so easy to be playful, sensual, vulnerable, fierce, spontaneous and sexual? You can open fully to all of life, the pleasurable and the painful, because, in reality, nothing's at stake.

Radiance Raising Ritual #4: *Commune in Nature*

Nothing shows you how trustworthy Life is better than a meditative walk in nature. This fourth ritual is to regularly go out into nature and consciously notice (that's the key, to really look) not only the harmony and balance of all living things, but the deep level of trust that exists in nature. While there is a life cycle, there's also deep trust that everything is unfolding perfectly and that everything is ultimately okay. Plants and animals come and go, and yet the bird, if you pay attention, trusts that Life will provide a worm and the trees trust that rain will come and the sun will shine. All of nature exists in harmony with and as a reflection of Perfection, and when you see nature with spiritual eyes, you recognize that you are a part of the Whole. The result of such communion with nature is that your inner tension relaxes and you can more fully trust and open to all of life—and even men!

Attraction Factors
1. Rank the 4 Bitch Blockers (Blaming, Believing, Busyness and Baggage) in terms of how negatively they're blocking your radiance.

2. Which "Radiance Raising Ritual" are you going to do first?

25

How to Raise Your Radiance, pt. 2

"Your yearning attracts and inspires love. If you allow your deepest yearning to show through your entire body, you will attract and inspire a deep man. He can truly see you, he can feel your deepest heart, and he can enter you completely. As if this were his last moment on earth with you, he is unafraid to lose everything in his full offering of love."

~ David Deida

Think of your radiance as being controlled by a dimmer light switch. The more you turn it, the brighter your light shines. That's exactly how it works with your Feminine radiance.

4 Bitch Brighteners

There are 4 ways you can "turn your dimmer switch" and brighten your "bitch-ness": Breath, Body, Beauty and Babes. Let's take these four one at a time.[66]

Bitch Brightener #1: Breath

The first way a woman can brighten her shine is by practicing conscious breathing. While everyone breathes, a radiant woman intentionally uses her breath to move energy through her body and keep her heart from closing down in fear.

In case you haven't noticed, being a radiant woman is scary. Being playful, sensual, vulnerable, spontaneous, fierce and sexual sounds great until you actually try to live that way! Then it becomes terrifying. And when we're scared, we hold our breath or it becomes very shallow. If we stop breathing long enough, we will physically turn blue; if a woman stops breathing long enough, she will spiritually turn "blue." Her radiance will be diminished and she will probably develop other problems in her body. So I

---

[66] These 4 "B's" will be discussed briefly, as were the 4 "B's" in the last chapter. If I were to fully explore them, this book would be as long as *War and Peace*! If you want more support in applying them to your life, perhaps one-on-one coaching is something you should consider.

want to talk about three aspects of conscious breathing: (1) How to breathe, (2) When to breathe, and (3) What to breathe.

(1) *How to breathe.* Perhaps you're aware of two simple yogic breathing poses called the "Cow" and the "Cat." They are perfect examples of conscious breathing.

Get on your hands and knees with your back flat and look straight down at the floor. As you begin to inhale, arch your back (caving it in like a cow) and lift your head toward the ceiling. Then, on the exhale, slowly go the other way until your back rolls up as far as it can, like a cat, and your chin tucks all the way down to your chest. You can go back and forth. It feels incredible. It would be a wonderful practice to do this first thing in the morning, right when you get out of bed.

This type of conscious breathing is what a radiant woman practices when she's scared. (Men too.) However, you don't have to get on your hands and knees to do it. (It might be weird to get on all fours when you're talking to some cute guy in public, don't you think?)

There's a mini, subtle version of the "Cow/Cat" pose, called the "Yes" breath, and it can be done without anyone knowing you're doing it. The breathing is done just as slowly and deeply, and the body still moves in the same basic way, but the movements are so subtle that no one will notice what you're doing. (It's called the "yes" breath because the head moves up and down.)

(2) *When to breathe.* When you feel scared, nervous or anxious, notice that your muscles will constrict and your stomach will clench. You'll stop breathing or your breath will be shallow and high up in your chest. The moment you notice that, do the "yes" breath (or the "Cow/Cat," if it's appropriate).

For example, imagine that a guy approaches you in public. Immediately one of your beliefs (aka, bitch blocker #2) flashes in your mind: "I bet this guy only wants sex." That thought will cause your stomach to clench and you might find it hard to breathe. You're scared. That's fine, just do the "yes" breath and open your heart to him. Assume he wants all of you until he proves otherwise.

(3) *What to breathe.* When you're talking to this guy, or even on a date, a radiant woman is not only practicing the "yes" breath to keep her heart from closing in fear, but she's using her breath to join their hearts together in love. Even if she has no romantic interest in a guy, a radiant woman stands for love and is filled with love. So anytime she meets a man (or any-

171

one, for that matter), what she's breathing is not air, but metaphorically, love. In a spiritual sense, she's feeling deeply into him and allowing his presence to enter her. She's communing, even though it's a casual conversation. She's inhaling the man's consciousness into her body and exhaling her love and light from her heart to his. This is radical openness and vulnerability and a man will feel it.

Now, there are degrees to which you can practice this depending on how intimate you'd like to be with a guy. If it's just the guy making your coffee at Starbucks, you can subtly breathe with him, and in just a moment of eye contact, because your heart is so wide open, you'll change his whole day. But if you're talking to someone you want to attract, or if you're on a date, you can offer your full devotional surrender, breathing him into your body and filling him with your love. He will see the openness in your eyes. That openness is radiance. What man could or would want to resist that?

Bitch Brightener #2: Body

There's a beautiful scene in the movie *Pleasantville* that perfectly illustrates how a woman's radiance is raised by her willingness to explore and experience bodily pleasure.

In the movie, as each character decides to live more authentically, their appearance is transformed from black and white to Technicolor. Every character's transformation has meaning, but it's the mother's transformation that illustrates this second "bitch brightener."

Since the woman has two kids in high school, we can guess that she's in her 40's. When we first meet her, she's in black and white, dull and gray. She is not a radiant woman. But then she discovers that her body has an incredible capacity for pleasure. Through masturbation, she gets in touch with her body so deeply that not only does the very color of her skin change, not only does she transform into this radiant, alive woman, but her body unleashes so much power and energy that it sets a tree on fire outside her house.[67] What a profound message to women.

A woman's power and radiance is ignited by her willingness and capacity to experience bodily pleasure.

---

[67] Here's the scene: http://bit.ly/1nwJ6rD

Now, sexuality is just one of the ways a radiant single woman does this and I would advise her to have a regular masturbation practice.[68] It brightens her shine and keeps her Feminine energy alive and flowing. But there are other body practices a woman can engage in regularly and I list a few of them below. Feel free to add to the list. A radiant woman gives herself permission to experience decadent amounts of pleasure in her body. It makes her feel alive and makes her shine like the sun.

(1) *Diet, Exercise, Hydration and Sleep.* Radiant women treat their physical bodies with respect. They are committed to each of these "4 pillars of physical health." She loves her body and takes care of it. How could she expect a man to love and respect her body if she doesn't? Now, I am not saying radiant women are all size 2's. Not at all. But I am saying every radiant woman takes care of herself.

(2) *Movement.* Beyond exercise, a radiant woman seeks to commune with life through moving her body. She's "water," not "banks," remember? She's flowing and moving, rarely static and still. In fact, meditation, as it's commonly practiced, is Masculine, and it's not a spiritual practice I advise for women who wish to brighten their shine. I'd rather women "meditate" by doing yoga, interpretive dance (or dance of any kind) or walking in nature. In other words, the Feminine communes through movement while the Masculine communes through stillness.

(3) *Body-Opening Practices.* I've already mentioned yoga, but radiant woman constantly tweak their bodies like a guy tweaks his car. She's always working on her "parts," if you will, by going to her gynecologist, getting mammograms and yearly check-ups from her regular doctor. But a radiant woman also takes advantage of non-traditional medical practices like massage, Reiki and acupuncture, while never ignoring the basics like bubble baths, stretching or sunbathing. In other words, a radiant woman tends to, and enjoys, her body.

(4) *Oprah's "Favorite Things."* I don't know if Oprah still does her "Favorite Things" segment, but a radiant woman is fully on board with the concept. She feels no guilt in having "guilty pleasures," because it's balanced by her overall diet and exercise commitment. Whether it's coffees, teas, chocolates, scents, soaps or shampoos, the radiant woman takes full responsibility for creating pleasure and joy in her life. She unapologetically

---

[68] Casual sex, in my experience and work with woman, does not brighten radiance, but diminishes it. Additionally, the encouragement to masturbate is directed at women only, for excessive ejaculation weakens a man's presence and power. This is one of the many ways in which the Masculine is different from the Feminine.

indulges in the simple (and not so simple things) in life that make her feel happy to be alive and living in a woman's body.

My coach, Diana, is a woman who coaches Fortune 500 CEO's and their leadership teams. It's obviously a very Masculine environment. But she's a radiant woman committed to her Femininity, and part of the way she counteracts all that Masculine influence, is that she has a morning practice where she finds something, usually online, that makes her cry. She wants to keep her heart soft and tender and not allow it to harden, which can happen because of all the Masculine energy with which she surrounds herself every day. So she makes the tears flow every morning. That's a woman committed to her Feminine energy.

Bitch Brightener #3: Beauty

The third practice that raises a woman's radiance is the commitment to beauty. She wants to commune, connect, converse, and frankly, "consummate" with Beauty. In other words, nothing makes her feel more alive and happy than when her heart is opened by some sensual experience. So a radiant woman is committed to surrounding herself with beautiful things and experiences that open her heart and allow her to give her deepest gifts to the world. What are these beautiful things? Well, they're highly individual. They're whatever has that effect on you.

It could be going to church and singing hymns; it could be rolling around in dew-drenched grass; it could be sitting on the porch watching the sun set or the rage of a violent thunderstorm. It could be a walk on the beach, or listening to your favorite music or a visit to the zoo, a museum or even a mall. It could be talking, exercising, gardening, painting, cooking, decorating, shopping or entertaining. It could be a new hairstyle or outfit or even something special like perfume, a facial or a mani-pedi.

The list is endless. The point is that radiant woman are deeply committed to keeping their hearts open to all of life and they do it through breath, body and beauty. But there's one more and most women overlook it, to their detriment.

Bitch Brightener #4: Babes

Radiant women are very particular about their friends, the kinds of women with whom they hang around. They want to surround themselves with women on the same radiant path, because they know that when you put a log on a burning fire, it catches fire too. Radiant women want to be on "fire," burning with radiance, openness and love. To do that, they seek out other radiant women and they're willing to walk away from those who are not committed to the same path. They realize that every "babe" they come in contact with either brightens their shine or diminishes it.

Because the Feminine gets lost in people, drama and feelings, as we said in a previous chapter, sometimes her compassionate heart keeps her from seeing that a particular relationship might be diminishing, rather than brightening, her radiance. Some people are committed to drama, suffering and victimhood. They might say they want help, but in reality, they don't want to take responsibility for their lives and make changes. They just want to whine about it and have you agree with their story. In other words, misery loves company. Sometimes, a woman expends a great deal of time and energy to save her "drowning" friend and one day she realizes that she's allowed herself to get sucked under too.

A radiant woman is constantly evaluating her relationships and making sure that they are supporting her deepest desire to open in radiant love.

So there are always two movements in a radiant woman's inner circle of friends. First, she's always letting go of those who aren't going where she's going, and secondly, she's always looking to join those who are.

How are your friendships right now? Are they lifting you up or are they pulling you down? What changes do you have to make so that your "log" catches fire and you burn as brightly as the sun?

Conclusion: *Team*mates and *Soul*mates

A couple of times in this book I've alluded to the fact that I was a professional golfer. I played on the PGA Tour, in major championships—all the stuff you see on TV. Well, one of the most important decisions a player at that level makes is who will be his caddy because they do a lot more than carry the clubs. The player and his caddy are actually teammates. A caddy helps with strategy and decision-making and sometimes even with the player's swing. In times of adversity, they talk a player "off the ledge" by using humor, encouragement or even a kick in the ass.

Because the caddy plays such a vital role, *the player picks someone based upon how much he thinks the caddy can help him succeed.* He needs the right teammate to bring out the best in him and help him get where he wants to go.

A good man chooses a woman for the exact same reason—to help him succeed. Remember, the Masculine's priority is his mission. A good man knows his life's purpose and he wants to achieve it, whether it's enlightenment or entrepreneurship. So he chooses a woman who he feels will best help him achieve that mission. Here is a crucial distinction:

> *A man chooses a woman to be his <u>teammate</u>;*
> *a woman chooses a man to be her <u>soulmate</u>*

Teammates and soulmates are very, very different things. Since the Feminine's priority is love, she chooses a partner based upon how well she believes he'll help her feel love, so she's choosing a *soul*mate. But a man chooses a woman to help him achieve his mission, so he's choosing a *team*mate.

When a woman knows how to be a teammate, a caddy if you will, she won't be single for long. When she knows how to support his deepest desire, he'll choose her. Likewise, when a man knows how to be a soulmate, he won't be single for long either. When he knows how to support her deepest desire, she'll choose him.

Now, how do you do that? Well, I just spent the last four chapters telling you! Being a radiant woman is being his teammate. When you're playful, sensual, vulnerable, fierce, spontaneous and sexual, that transmission of Feminine energy will light up his life, renew his soul and inspire his mission.

There's a scene in the movie, *As Good As It Gets* that powerfully captures this. Jack Nicholson plays a neurotic moron who suffers from obsessive/compulsive disorder. He's on a date with Helen Hunt at a nice restaurant, and he makes another one of his insulting comments, and she's furious. She demands that he give her a compliment or she's walking out. Nicholson obliges and starts stammering, saying that since he met her, he's started to take his medication for what he calls his "ailment." Hunt is confused. She doesn't see how him taking pills is a compliment. It's at that point that he says, "You make me want to be a better man." [69] Her radiance, her energy, simply the way she *moves*, inspires, motivates and challenges him to be a better man.

Do *that* and you won't be single for long.

When I introduced this section, I quoted author, David Deida. I'm going to share the same quote again now, for perhaps its last sentence, which I've italicized, will mean more to you now than it may have back then.

---

[69] Here's the scene: http://bit.ly/1sElzEo

"If a man has a Masculine sexual essence, then his priority is his mission, his direction toward greater release, freedom, and consciousness. If a woman has a Feminine sexual essence, then her priority is the flow of love in her life, including her relationship with a man whom she can totally trust, in body, emotion, mind, and spirit. *Man and woman must support each other in their priorities if the relationship is going to serve them both.*"

Attraction Factors

1. What specific action steps are you going to take in regards to the 4 Bitch Brighteners discussed?

26

Five Kinds of Super Men

What makes Superman a hero is not that he has power, but that he has the wisdom and the maturity to use the power wisely."

~ Christopher Reeve

There are many different kinds of men in the world. There's "Mr. Mom," "Prince Charming," "Peter Pan," "Macho Men," "Yes Men," "Bullies," "Partiers," "Players," "New Age Wimps," "Frat Boys," "Bad Boys," "Nice boys," "Mama's Boys," "Playboys," and "Boy Toys."

What kind of man are you?

What kind of man am I?

Over the next three chapters, I want to discuss what it means to be Masculine—in the best sense of the word.[70] There is a lot of man bashing in the world these days, and while some of it's unfair, much of it's not. Far too often we men (yes, I include myself) are unfocused, egotistical and untrustworthy, mired in mediocrity and passivity, falling far short of our divine callings as men. In other words, too often we are not Super Men, but some lesser version of our true identity.

My premise is that although men have very different backgrounds, beliefs, nationalities, races, ages, personalities and sexual orientations…

There is a universal Masculine way, that when discovered and displayed, makes a man irresistible to radiant women.

In other words, when a man shuns the controlling, carousing or collapsing versions of Masculinity, and instead aligns his heart and life with the directed, disciplined and divine versions, women will line up to be with him.

---

[70] These next 3 chapters are directed at men but I strongly encourage women not to skip them. Knowing the potential of a man is a key step in attracting him.

5 Kinds of Super Men

It's fair to say that we, as a society, have been obsessed with superheroes. Whether it's Batman, Spider-Man, The Hulk, Hercules, Thor, Captain America or Iron Man, to name a few, it seems we've always been fascinated by the Masculine superhero archetype. And if there's one super hero that stands out among all the others, if there's a quintessential icon of Masculinity, it has to be Superman. He's "faster than a speeding bullet, more powerful than a locomotive and able to leap tall buildings in a single bound."

Men have always fantasized about being Superman. There's something special about having a secret identity as "a mild mannered reporter," and at the first sign of trouble, we rip open our shirts, revealing a big red "S" on our chests so that the world can see our true identity.

Well, that's not a fantasy.

If you rip open the shirt of ANY man
you will find a big red "S" on his chest.

It just depends on what that "S" stands for.

There are five different kinds of super men: (1) The Super *Simple* Man, (2) The Super *Sensitive* Man, (3) The Super *Successful* Man, (4) The Super *Sexual* Man, or (5) The *Superior* man.

The fifth one, The Superior Man, is our divine calling as men and the next chapter is devoted exclusively to it. But before we can discuss what it means to be Masculine in the best sense of the word, we first have to come to grips with 4 counterfeit versions of Masculinity, for they are each barriers to attracting lasting love.

(1) The Super *Simple* Man

This is the traditional, conservative, strong, silent type epitomized by the 1950's male. It's the husband in the movie, *Pleasantville*, who comes home from work and says, "Honey, I'm home…Where's my dinner?" He's a simple man, scoffing at "liberal bullshit," believing "men should be men and women should be women." He's the breadwinner, the king of his castle, and his wife is the submissive, stay-at-home housewife. His children are to be seen and not heard and he certainly doesn't change diapers.

Emotionally, he's distant and detached. Anger is the only emotion he feels, and in his family, he's the only one allowed to feel it. Sexually, he's mechanical and missionary—he "gets on, gets off and gets to sleep". He's very religious, but not spiritual, and politically he's republican, anti-gay marriage and hawkish.

Radiant women dislike this guy because he's a caveman, but some "regular" women still desire him because he's a stable provider. The Super *Simple* Man is best represented by Archie Bunker, or nowadays, Bill O'Reilly.

(2) The Super *Sensitive* Man

The Super *Sensitive* Man is the exact opposite of the *Simple* man in almost every way. The sensitive man is extremely in touch with his Feminine side. He is able to experience and express all his emotions (except anger—he suppresses that because it might hurt someone's feelings). He's a sweet, soft, sincere, super-nice guy who wouldn't hurt a fly.

The Super *Sensitive* Man is egalitarian, liberal and spiritual, but not religious. He may enjoy tango or salsa dancing, yoga or spin classes, and he has a ton of female friends. Oh, and he'll definitely change diapers. Sexually, he's gentle and unselfish, wondering "was it good for you?" and seeking simultaneous orgasms. He's also health conscious, perhaps even a vegetarian, preferring wine and cheese to cheeseburgers and beer.

Most women really like the sensitive guy because he's a great friend and he feels safe, yet strangely, they don't feel sexually attracted to him. He's a bit "light," wimpy and collapsible, so women, and especially radiant women, can't trust him completely nor surrender to him sexually. Therefore, the Super *Sensitive* Man ends up in the dreaded "Friend Zone."

Culturally, he's best represented by the likes of Phil Donahue, Richard Gere or Anderson Cooper.

(3) The Super *Successful* Man

In the 1987 movie, *Wall Street,* Gordon Gekko uttered the famous line, "Greed is good."[71] More recently, Leonardo DiCaprio played Jordan Belfort in the movie, *The Wolf of Wall Street*, another greedy, unprincipled businessman.[72] These two are iconic symbols of our third counterfeit version of true Masculinity, The Super *Successful* Man.

This kind of man is driven, power hungry, materialistic and cutthroat. He's an uber-competitive, win-at-all-costs, take no prisoners kind of guy. He lives by the adage, "Winning isn't everything; it's the only thing." He

---

[71] Here's the scene if you're unfamiliar with it: http://bit.ly/1da1q4J

[72] Here's the trailer to the movie: http://bit.ly/JwsA8o

plays by his own rules and will do whatever it takes to win and succeed, including lying, taking advantage of others or stabbing them in the back.

He may be religious, but that's only to enhance and control his image. In reality, his god is money, fame and success. If he doesn't have a mansion, a Rolex and a Ferrari, his life's purpose is to get them. Relationally, he has a trophy wife and a mistress, and sex is about conquest and/or stress relief.

Radiant women are not interested in this guy because he's disconnected from his divine core, but some women are attracted to his money and power. However, they're quickly disappointed when they learn that the true love of his life is money and it will never be them.

The Super *Successful* Man is best represented by the likes of Donald Trump and Michael Jordan.

(4) The Super *Sexual* Man

The final counterfeit version of the divine Masculine is The Super *Sexual* Man. He's smooth, cocky, witty and charming. If there was ever a guy that has "game," it's him. He's impeccably dressed, at least decent looking, always physically fit and drives a nice car. He's a player, a ladies man and an eternal bachelor. Ryan Gosling brilliantly portrays this persona in the 2011 movie, *Crazy, Stupid, Love.*[73]

The Super *Sexual* Man is great in the sack. He really knows his way around a woman's body, but he has absolutely no clue about her heart (or his). Probably a sex addict, his penis and his heart are miles apart, which allows him to "have sex," but never "make love." Underneath the suave exterior is a deeply insecure man who fears real intimacy, and ultimately, he hates women. They are nothing more than objects and notches in his ego's belt.

A radiant woman sees that the sexual man is shallow, superficial and scared of truly claiming a woman's heart, and therefore, like all the other counterfeit versions of Masculinity, she feels compassion for him, but no real interest in him. However, other women do fall for such men but they end up getting their hearts broken.

Of the four counterfeit types of Masculinity, the sexual man is perhaps the most destructive and damaging one of all. When a woman allows herself to be seduced by the sexual man's charm, and then comes to realize she's just another notch in his belt, her heart closes and she's less able to trust

---

[73] This is a collection of his scenes in the movie: http://bit.ly/1nwksY7

men in the future. In other words, his "hit it and quit it" ways create wounds that may never heal.

Hugh Hefner, James Bond, Tiger Woods and many male Rap artists are iconic symbols of The Super *Sexual* Man.

Conclusion

What kind of "S" do you wear on your chest?

Frankly, I can relate to all of them. *In fact, I have been every single one of those "super men."* Even now, after all the spiritual work I've done, I notice little pieces of those 4 counterfeit versions still hanging around in my consciousness. So although I describe them harshly, I'm actually not judging you, me, or any man for being caught in one or more of these counterfeit versions of Masculinity, because…

Our childhoods, churches, classrooms and culture have conditioned most of us to be either simple, sensitive, successful or sexual men—or some combination of them.

The intention here is not to shame men (there's enough of that going on), but merely to point out that we are capable of being so much more. Underneath our egos and fears, we are Superior Men and it's time we start living like it. Our world is in desperate need of men committed to animating the divine Masculine in their lives and women are hungering and hoping to be penetrated by the deep presence of a Superior Man.

Radiant women are sick and tired of the controlling, collapsing, disengaged or dehumanizing versions of Masculinity and they yearn for a man they can deeply trust.

You are that guy and so am I.

Now that we know what it does NOT mean to be Masculine, we can turn our attention toward what it does mean. The next chapter describes the heart and soul of a Superior Man, a man women want and the world desperately needs.

Attraction Factors

1. Which one of the four counterfeit versions of Masculinity can you most identify with?

2. Give an example of how you have been a simple, sensitive, successful or sexual guy and the effects it has had on your love life and the particular woman involved.

3. Do you need to have a completion conversation with a woman as a result of what you just described? In other words, do you need to go back to her and own up to the kind of guy you were with her? (This is something a superior man would definitely do.)

— 27 —

The Measure of a Superior Man

"The superior man is unabashedly Masculine—he is purposeful, confident and directed, living his chosen way of life with deep integrity and humor...He is dedicated to incarnating love on this earth, through his work and his sexuality."

~ David Deida

This chapter presents a vision of the divine Masculine, one that preserves our individuality and uniqueness as men and yet binds us together in a common calling.

What you are about to read is very challenging and very few men will be interested in fully committing their lives to it. They will either continue pursuing one of the four Masculine personas I just described, or they will be content to lead a mediocre life where their life's purpose amounts to nothing more than "gettin' paid and gettin' laid."

Most men are too scared to confront themselves with questions like, what do I stand for, who am I and what am I here to give? Instead, they settle for a safe and secure existence, spending their lives chasing their own tails, or skating through life, "fat, drunk and stupid,"[74] unwilling to live at their edge and make a real difference in both the world and women's lives.

Yet, I believe *some* men are willing to live by a transcendent vision, something not found in a Faith, nor forwarded to them by their fathers, but forged in the fires of their own fearless search for Truth. These are the kinds of men radiant women want and the world desperately needs.

The Superior Man[75]

---

[74] Here's the scene from the classic movie, *Animal House*: http://bit.ly/1Fobmm0

[75] I have created an entire video-based eCourse on the subject of what it means to be the kind of man women want and it goes into far more depth than I can here. Here's a link to a 4-minute trailer on *The Superior Man: Becoming the Man Every Woman Wants and the World Desperately Needs*

When a man devotes himself to developing and displaying the following 3 aspects of the divine Masculine in his life, he can truly be called A Superior Man, and he can pretty much have any woman he wants.

WHAT IS A SUPERIOR MAN?

Clarity of Consciousness
The Superior Man knows his life's purpose and is living it with integrity, persistence and humor

Strength of Presence
The Superior Man has the desire and the ability to remain undistracted and uncollapsible in the midst of his partner's Feminine energy

Openness of Heart
The Superior Man is aware of his inner emotional landscape and he shares it candidly and consistently with his partner

This is a critical moment for every man reading this chapter because I'm betting these three things don't surprise you that much. In fact, you've probably heard of them (or some version of them) before. Therefore, I'm afraid you might think you're actually living this way already.

You're not.

That might be a presumptuous and outrageous thing to say, but I stand by it for two reasons. First, think of these 3 qualities on a scale of 1 to 10, where a "1" means a man is clueless in regards to them, a "5" means he's average, and a "10" would mean he's truly a superior man.

I can count on one hand the number of men I have known that I would consider 10's. In fact, I rarely meet a man above a "5," so I seriously doubt you are. On my best day, I would only give myself an "8," and that might be generous.[76] Don't overestimate yourself and think you are a superior man

---

[76] I am now 54 and I spent the first 45 years of my life as a "3," at best.

simply because you've heard of these ideas before and think you understand them.

Secondly, men who rate "5" or above are rarely single for long. There are far too many distant, distracted, disengaged and dark men in the world (I was one of them for a long time), and when a guy is merely above average, much less superior, he gets gobbled up pretty quickly. In other words:

If you are embodying these three things to some degree in your life, you wouldn't be single and you wouldn't be reading this book.

(1) Clarity of Consciousness—*The superior man knows his life's purpose and he lives it with integrity, persistence and humor.*

In the popular TV show, *Shark Tank*, aspiring entrepreneurs pitch their products to a group of multi-millionaires hoping that one of the 5 "Sharks" will believe in them enough to not only invest money in their venture, but actually become business partners with them.

Now, the 5 multi-millionaires (and billionaire, in the case of Mark Cuban) are not called "Sharks" for nothing. They ruthlessly evaluate the entrepreneurs that come on the show, and if they can't clearly articulate their business plan, their marketing strategy and their financial condition, the sharks tear them to shreds and refuse to do business with them. However, when the entrepreneurs *can* demonstrate that they know what they want to do and how they plan to do it, the Sharks actually fight with one another, and even try to outbid each other for the opportunity to go into business with the entrepreneur.

Guys, that's *EXACTLY* what's happening every time you meet a woman. Whether you know it or not (and most guys don't), she is just like those Sharks, evaluating whether or not she should "invest" in you and become your "business partner." If you can clearly articulate who you are, what you're doing with your life and how you plan to get there, she'll basically throw herself at you, just like the Sharks do. But if you can't demonstrate where your life is headed and how you plan to get there, she will refuse to do "business" with you.

Radiant women are looking for men with what I call, *Clarity of Consciousness.* Yes, chemistry is important to them, *but what they're really interested in is how well you are living your entire life—financially, emotionally, physically and spiritually.* She wants to know if you have your shit together, what your goals are and what your plan is to achieve them. Why would she want to be a part of a life not being lived well, for when it comes right down to it...

A woman wants to know if she can trust you with her life.

Yes, she can take care of herself, and yes, she has her own goals—a radiant woman is no "damsel in distress"—but in reality, being your woman means she's putting her life in your hands. *Even if she makes more money than you, she longs to relax in the demonstration of your direction, which extends to every part of your life.* Do you get that? If you aren't navigating your life with clarity, integrity and intentionality, if you can't articulate why you're alive and what you're trying to do with your one and only life, why in hell would she hook up with you? She'd be a fool, wouldn't she? And radiant women are not fools.

Do you want to know why most men get dismissed, dumped or divorced? Well, it's for the same reason the entrepreneurs on *Shark Tank* get rejected: They lack Clarity of Consciousness. Now, a whole book could be written on this subject, but let me give you a couple of practical examples of what lacking Clarity of Consciousness looks like:

- If you don't like your job or career, and you're not doing anything about it because it's comfortable and pays well, you're out of integrity and she won't be able to trust you.
- If you are blaming any problem in your life on someone else, be it your parents, an ex, your boss, your kids, your health, or the economy, your victim mentality will make her unable to trust you.
- If you have always had a dream of doing a particular thing with your life (e.g., writing a book, starting a business, climbing a mountain, etc., etc.), but have abandoned it because of fear of failure, family pressure, lack of funds or challenging circumstances, your passivity and weakness will make her unable to trust you.
- If you're the kind of guy who's "workin' for the weekend," like *Loverboy* sang back in the 80's, meaning, if your life's purpose is to enjoy your hobbies, watch sports on TV or get drunk on the weekends, she won't be able to trust you, nor should she. Why would she put her life in the hands of a man who's committed to such a trivial existence?
- If you're constantly changing jobs or careers, bouncing from one thing to another, your lack of clarity, focus and perseverance will make her unable to trust you.

- If you are physically, financially or emotionally "out of shape" and a mess, your lack of discipline will make her unable to trust you. If you can't manage your life, how could you manage hers?
- If you can't articulate exactly what your life will look like in 1, 5 and 10 years from now, including the family structure you want, the career you'll have, the amount of money you plan to make and even the place you plan to live, that lack of clarity will make her unable to trust you.

Sugar Daddies?

When I talk to men about these things, they seem to think I'm saying women want "sugar daddies." That's not it at all. Yes, some women are obsessed with a man's bucks, just as some men are obsessed with a woman's boobs (they reflect the same state of consciousness), but radiant women and superior men are never that narrowly focused. Just as a superior man is interested in a woman's energetic radiance, which has nothing to do with her bra size, so a radiant woman is interested in a man's clarity of consciousness, which has nothing to do with his wallet size.

For example, a man who teaches in an elementary school won't make huge dollars. Yet if he feels like he's been put on the earth to invest in kid's lives and to be the solid male role model that so many children lack—to a radiant woman—that's HOT! He knows his life's purpose and he's living it. He has Clarity of Consciousness. Even though he'll never make a ton of money, she respects and admires his purpose and the way he's living his life and that's sexy. That's a guy she can trust because he knows who he is and what he's about.

Perhaps my most memorable session with my coach, Diana, was when I was single and complaining to her about how some woman gave me her number but then ignored my calls. At that time, my life's purpose was basically to find a woman. I wasn't up to much more than that. So Diana interrupted my whining and asked me in an angry, challenging tone, "Roy, why *should* she call you back? What do you have to offer her? Seems to me that your life is about is getting laid. Why would she want to be with you? What's your mission in life?"

I was livid. I went on a five-minute screaming rant using every four-letter word imaginable, telling her how wrong she was. But in reality, she wasn't wrong. She was spot on. My life, at that point, was about nothing more than finding a woman, and the radiant ones weren't giving me the time of day, much less their hearts, because I was lacking Clarity of Consciousness.

There's nothing less attractive to a radiant woman than a single man whose life purpose is about finding her.

Now, guys, I know you're reading this book because you want to attract lasting love. *But what are you attracting her to?* That's the question. What is it that you're inviting her to be a part of? What's your plan? Where are you going? What are you trying to do with your life and how well are you living it?

Right now, in this moment, if I asked you why are you alive and what will your life look like in 5 years, could you answer me?

You will never have a radiant woman until you can.

Do not fool yourself. Every woman is a "Shark." She's asking, why are you alive and how well are you living your purpose? If you don't have this kind of Clarity of Consciousness, you'll never attract a radiant woman. And if you don't have it, the next chapter will help you find it.

(2) Strength of Presence—*The superior man has the desire and the ability to remain undistracted and uncollapsible in the midst of his partner's Feminine energy*

Are you strong enough to be her man? Can you handle her, and the full force of her Feminine flow? Not many men can—*or even want to.* But a superior man relishes the challenge she presents and he's emotionally strong enough to contain her wild radiance.

Remember, as Meredith Brooks put it so perfectly, a radiant woman is a "bitch." She's an emotional, unpredictable, chaotic creature. She's supposed to be that way. The question is, are your "river banks" wide and deep enough to contain and guide her flow? In other words, can you stand in the midst of the storm of her emotional volatility and remain uncollapsible and present? If you can, you will be rewarded with a radiance so bright that she will light up your life and make you ecstatically happy to be alive. If you can't, your love life will never be satisfying. Clarity of Consciousness is about how well you're navigating your life...

Strength of Presence is about how well you can navigate her life— emotionally, spiritually and sexually.

Clarity is about "where and how" (*where* are you going and *how* are you going to get there), while Strength is about "here and now." Can you be

100% present in the midst of her mood and mania, remaining undistracted, grounded and uncollapsible, or do you run, retreat or retaliate when she's being a "bitch?"

NFL Quarterbacks

The best NFL Quarterbacks (Tom Brady, Drew Brees, Aaron Rogers, Peyton Manning) are perfect illustrations of what it means to have Strength of Presence. What makes those QBs so good is not so much their knowledge of defenses or even their arm strength, it's their ability stand in the pocket, in the midst of chaos, confusion, duress and danger—*and know what to do*. The best QBs have what's called, *Pocket Presence*. They don't run or panic at the first sign of pressure. They stand in there, completely aware of everything that's happening on the field, and make the right decision, even though they know they're going to get hit.

A superior man is just like a great NFL Quarterback (and almost as rare!). He, too, has "pocket presence." When things get crazy, confusing and chaotic, he doesn't collapse. He "stands in there," unafraid and undistracted—completely present—*and he knows what to do*, which might be anything from listening to her, to holding her, to dancing with her, to ravishing her.

Everything a superior man does with women, whether they're friends or lovers, is designed to serve Love and Freedom. His actions are never for his benefit; they're for her benefit (actually for Love's benefit). A superior man is constantly asking how he can use his presence to direct a woman, or their relationship, toward Love and Freedom. This, at times, is more challenging than playing Quarterback in the NFL!

Collapsible Men

There are 4 ways a man collapses when being "rushed" by the Feminine. In the next chapter, I'll give you some presence practices, but for now, let's look at how we collapse:

(A) Fix. When a woman is upset, frustrated or just generally emotional, most men see that as a problem to be fixed. On one hand, this is understandable, since the Masculine expresses love by fixing problems. It's what we do.[77] However, a superior man knows that when a woman is emotional *she doesn't need to be fixed; she needs to be felt.*

---

[77] This video clip called, *It's Not About the Nail*, is absolutely hilarious. If there was just one clip you listen to in this book, make it this one: http://bit.ly/1wewpSM

After she's felt a man's presence, it might be appropriate to recommend a solution, but normally, the knee-jerk tendency to fix is less about what she needs and more about what we need (their flow can be exhausting). In moments of stress, worry, frustration or confusion, what she needs is our uncollapsible, undistracted, loving presence so that she can open in Love. And that presence is hardly ever verbal; rather, it's physical (as we'll see in the next chapter).

(B) Flee. The second way men collapse is by fleeing the scene. Like a QB fleeing the pocket and running for his life, we run away from a woman's emotional expression. We do this by physically leaving the situation (or retreating into our "man cave") or by telling her to go talk about it to her girlfriends or family members. What we're basically saying is "I can't handle you. My banks aren't wide or deep enough to handle your flow. Go find someone with better and bigger banks than mine." (This is usually when a woman finds a new man.)

(C) Faint. Sometimes we don't physically leave a situation, we emotionally leave. Meaning, we're physically in her presence, but we're not emotionally there. We check out, numb out, tune out or veg out, usually by drifting off in our heads, watching TV, drinking, surfing the Internet, staying busy or even attempting to change the subject. When a woman nags and complains about a man, it's usually because he's "fainted" in the relationship. A superior man takes nagging and complaining as a wake up call, an emotional "smelling salt," shocking him to be more alert and present.

(D) Force. The final way a man collapses and reveals his weakness is by being a bully and forcing a woman into submission, either by raising his voice, threatening to leave or even physically hitting her or destroying property. The tough guy is actually a weak guy, unable to contain the uncontrollable nature of both women and world. This is the football player, Ray Rice, and sadly, far too many other men.

Pole Dancing

When a man has Clarity of Consciousness, his life is governed and ruled by the eternal. He knows "God's" purpose for his life. When a man has Strength of Presence, his life is grounded and rooted in the temporal. In other words, he's securely attached to heaven and earth, God and ground. When a man is both clear and present, a woman can relax, dance and play, because he's so incredibly trustable.

In this sense, a superior man is like a stripper's pole. In order for a woman to wildly, and erotically dance on the pole (double entendre intended), it must be securely fastened to the ceiling and the ground. If it's not, it will collapse under the force of her dance.

I know, guys, that you want a woman to "dance on your pole" and on your entire life—and she wants that too! The question is this: Is your pole sturdy, secure and strong enough for her to do that, or will you collapse under the force of her Feminine flow? Are you a man who's living with Clarity of Consciousness and Strength of Presence?

Are you beginning to see why you aren't attracting really good women? The bar is set high. Radiant women want (and deserve) superior men. They won't settle for mediocrity. But if these first two aspects of the divine Masculine weren't challenging enough for you, perhaps this last one will be.

(3) Openness of Heart— *This man is aware of his inner emotional landscape and shares it candidly and consistently with his partner*

When I speak of Openness of Heart, let me assure you that I'm not trying to turn you into a woman. The goal here is not to become a "girly man," someone who watches Oprah, enjoys chick flicks and relishes the opportunity to talk about his feelings. In fact, radiant women don't expect us to be like them emotionally, nor do they want us to be. What's sexy about the Masculine is its ability to be uncollapsible, focused and steady in the midst of emotion and chaos, not be derailed by it. They don't want a man who's going to fall apart. In other words...

> ### Radiant women want a ROCK,
> ### but they want him to be REAL too

They want us to be stable and strong, but they don't want to be in a relationship with the "Tin Man" either. They know we have a heart and they know we have feelings. In other words, they know there's something going on inside of us and they want to be a part of it.[78] Yes, women are extremely attracted to the clarity of our lives and they're turned on by our ability to be physically and emotionally present with *their* emotional flow, but they also want to be present with our reality as well.

Having said that, the emotional realm is NOT a man's forte for at least two reasons. First, the Masculine, by definition, is naturally more equipped to focus than feel, and we've talked at length about that. But secondly, and

---

[78] Sometimes, a woman gets more than she's bargained for as Will Ferrell hilariously shows in this clip from *Old School*: http://bit.ly/1nwJiHn

more importantly, most guys have had very little encouragement and even less training on the emotional side of life. We've been told, "big boys don't cry," "don't be such a pussy," and not to be "scare-y cats." So most men have either suppressed their emotions or disowned them altogether. Therefore, when a woman asks a man what he's feeling, he often says, "I don't know," and he's probably telling the truth. He really doesn't know.

So, although our goal is not to become like women, we do need to be emotionally smarter than a 5th grader if we want to relate to the Feminine and attract lasting love. Now, a full discussion of emotional intelligence is far beyond the scope of this book, but let me discuss a couple of basics here, and in the next chapter, I'll give some practical how-to's.[79]

The Five Feelings

There are literally hundreds of words that describe feelings, but they all fall into 5 basic categories. For example, the words "frustrated," "annoyed" or "irritated" are all forms of anger. So here's a list of the five primary feelings, what they mean and where they're usually felt in the body.

Anger. When we feel angry it means *something needs to be stopped.* It's an energy that establishes and enforces a boundary. It can be used to serve love or ego, and therefore, it can be healthy or destructive. It's normally felt in the upper back, neck and jaw, which is why we say, "you're such a pain in the neck."

Scared. When we feel scared it means *something needs to be known.* Fear always is a response to the unknown and it drives us to ask important questions of others or ourselves. It's normally felt in the stomach, which is why we say, "I've got butterflies in my stomach."

Sad. When we feel sad it means *something needs to be released.* Sadness arises when we resist the impermanent nature of life and hold on to that which is passing away, be it a person, a job or any other transient aspect of life. It's normally felt in the chest, throat and behind the eyes, which is why we say, "I'm all choked up," or "My heart is broken."

Joy. When we feel joy it means *something needs to be celebrated.* In our culture, we really don't celebrate well. We immediately begin thinking about or planning for the next event or situation. Joy is normally felt as an overall tingling and upwardly rising energy, which is why we stand and throw our arms up into the air at a sporting event.

---

[79] All of what follows is good for women too. While women are more comfortable with the emotional realm than men are, they too can learn to handle their emotions more consciously.

Sexual Feelings. When we feel sexual, it means *something needs to be created*. Sex is not only the procreative urge, but it's also the creative urge behind art, music, writing or even the creation of a business. Far too many people waste their sexual energy on meaningless sex and don't know that it often signals that they are being urged to "birth" something new into the world. This energy is normally felt in the body's erogenous zones: breasts, mouth, and genitals.

Avoidance Strategies

It's not much of an exaggeration to say that the emotional realm scares the shit out of most men. The idea of "revealing rather than concealing" or "living out loud" feels foreign and uncomfortable, to say the least. We'd rather do almost anything other than talk about our feelings, especially if we think we might face ridicule, rejection or retribution for them.

So rather than simply feeling those 5 feelings and then candidly expressing them in a consistent fashion, we often choose to avoid them, and we do so in the following 6 ways:

Distraction. Instead of feeling our feelings, many men distract themselves by watching TV, surfing the net, masturbating, exercising, working, etc. What's your favorite way to distract yourself from what you're feeling? Mine is *ESPN*.

Medicate. Another favorite way men avoid their feelings is to medicate themselves with their drug of choice, which might be watching porn, drinking, gambling, getting high, eating, smoking, etc. What's your drug of choice when you want to numb a feeling? Mine is *Grey Goose*.

Analyze. Many men who are interested in personal growth try to figure out why they feel a certain way. This is probably my most common avoidance strategy. It seems healthy, but it's actually not. When we try to figure things out, we're still not actually feeling our feelings; we're up in our heads, subtly avoiding our direct experience.

Blame. One of our favorite avoidance strategies is to blame others for how we feel. On the surface this seems like a step in the right direction, because we are feeling and expressing, even though it's negative. But in fact, we're focusing outward, abandoning our direct experience and talking about someone else and what they did or didn't do. So, in effect, we're still avoiding our feelings.

Vent. Like blaming, when we vent, it appears that we're feeling our feelings, but we're not because we aren't actually contacting what's happening in our bodies, we're simply looking for someone who will listen to

194

and agree with our story. Telling a story is very different from feeling a feeling.

Spiritualize. Perhaps the sneakiest way people avoid their feelings is to explain them away with spiritual platitudes like "God is in control," "This too shall pass," or "Everything happens for a reason." Sometimes people even quote scripture. The reason this is dangerous is because there's some truth to the platitudes and the scripture verses. However, spiritualizing is a way of rescuing yourself from feeling the "negative" feelings, and therefore, it's destructive to your emotional health.

Wanted: Superior Men

So, that is the measure of a superior man. He is clear and on-purpose in every area of his life; his presence in the world and with women is strong, undistracted and uncollapsible—which makes him a "rock"—and yet he's real and open about his feelings and emotions.

Women lay awake at night fantasizing about a man like this, fearing that they'll never meet him.

It's a cliché, but you *can* be the man of her dreams. It's extremely challenging, but you can be a man of Clarity, Presence and Openness. And when you align yourself with these 3 divine Masculine qualities you can pretty much have any woman you want, and if you remain committed to being this kind of man, she will never leave you.

Now that we've established what a superior man is, we can begin talking about how to develop these qualities in our lives. The next chapter explains practical things you can do to be more superior in each of these three aspects of life.

Attraction Factors

1. Do you want to devote your life to being a clear, present, open man? In other words, are you willing to do whatever it takes to be a superior man?

2. On a scale of 1-10, how would the last 3 women in your life rate you concerning Clarity of Consciousness, Strength of Presence and Openness of Heart?

3. Which one of the 3 aspects of a superior man do you need to work on the most?

— 28 —

The Superior Man In Action

"Your Masculine gift is to know where you are, where you want to be, and what you need to do to get there. If you don't know one of these, then you need to discover it by any means necessary. This vision is, essentially, the basic gift you have to offer women and the world."

~ David Deida

One of my most vivid memories on the PGA Tour was when I played in the 1988 FedEx/St. Jude Memphis Classic. It wasn't memorable because of the way I played (I don't even remember); it was memorable because I got to fly a 747 Jumbo Jet in FedEx's flight simulator. Well, that's not really true. I *crashed* a 747 Jumbo Jet in their flight simulator—about 5 times!

FedEx is headquartered in Memphis and they have a state-of-the-art flight simulator for their pilots to practice in. It's exactly like a real cockpit and they can program the computer so that a pilot can take off or land at any airport in the world and in any weather or emergency situation.

Getting to fly this thing was one of the coolest things I've ever done, and even though I crashed repeatedly, I was taught something about being a man that I will never forget. Here's what happened:

I was the pilot and my former wife was the copilot. The instructor stood behind us describing the instruments and programming the computer. To make a long story short, I was okay taking off, but when I got in the air, I couldn't get the hang of turning the damn thing. You don't turn a plane like you turn a car (how was I supposed to know that?), and so I kept overturning and rolling the plane upside down...and crashing.

Now, when you're about to crash, it feels real (except for the death part). All hell breaks loose. My wife is screaming, "Roy, you're crashing!" I'm like, "No shit Sherlock!" The instructor is yelling, "Level out! Level out!" I'm yelling back at him, "How! I don't know *HOW*!"

It's chaos, sheer pandemonium. Horns are going off, the plane starts shaking, and a voice blares, "Terrain! Terrain! Terrain!" When you hit the ground the simulator shakes violently and the instructor deadpans, "You just killed everyone on board. Nice job."

196

At first this was pretty funny, but after the 5th time of crashing and burning, the instructor could tell I was lost. As I was rolling the plane over—again—and I will never forget this as long as I live, he reached over my shoulder and grabbed the Yoke (that's what a plane's steering wheel is called) and I, of course, let go.

Calmly, he said, "Roy, like this…" and with a quick jerk and a twist, all of which took about one second, the plane leveled off and flew perfectly. The shaking stopped, the horns stopped blaring and both my wife and the plane quit yelling at me.

That was, without question, the most powerful demonstration of Masculine energy I've ever experienced. The instructor was a "Superior Man" because in the midst of chaos and confusion, he reached in, took control and "saved" our lives.

As a superior single man, you must do the same thing. You must "grab the yoke" by bringing your divine Masculine energy to bear on how you (1) Live your life, (2) Lead your relationship, and (3) Love your woman. Let's get very practical and describe what that means.

(1) Live Your Life—Clarity of Consciousness

Author Sam Keen wrote, *"There are two questions a man must ask himself: The first is 'Where am I going?' and the second is 'Who will go with me?' If you ever get these questions in the wrong order you are in trouble."*

We've already talked about how important it is for a man to know his deepest purpose. Nothing is more painful to the Masculine soul than not having clarity as to what his life is about. And nothing is less attractive to a radiant woman than a man who's wandering aimlessly through life. If she's going to get onboard a man's "train," she has to know where it's headed. If you cannot clearly articulate the goal of your life and what your plan is to achieve it, a radiant woman will not be able to trust you. Not many men realize that this is THE issue that's keeping them single.

Therefore, you must live *YOUR* life, which means discovering your deepest purpose and then devoting yourself to achieving it. I want to point you towards 3 ways you can discover your purpose: Solitude/Austerity, forming a Purpose Posse and reading Authors of Aspiration. I've done each of them at various stages of my life. They are powerful practices for finding your purpose.

Solitude and Austerity. The first way to discover your life's purpose and be a man who has Clarity of Consciousness is to isolate yourself from all the normal comforts and distractions of life and sit in absolute silence and solitude until you begin to get a clear sense of what you're supposed to do with your life. This may mean anything from sitting alone in your home for days on end, without human contact or any use of electronic devices, to renting a cabin in the woods. The form doesn't matter; the solitude and austerity does.

This method has been, perhaps, the primary way men have found and clarified their purpose over the centuries. Jesus did this very thing right before his public ministry began. He went into the wilderness for 40 days and 40 nights and wrestled with his "demons" and determined who he was and what he stood for. You can trace the power and effectiveness in his life to that "vision quest" and if you want to be a superior man, as he was, you may need to follow in his steps.

Purpose Posse. The second way a man discovers his life's purpose is to form what I call a Purpose Posse. This is a group of 2-3 *superior* men who are willing to create a sacred and intense short-term space of support and accountability while you search for your truth. This can be extremely powerful in a man's life if, and only if, he chooses men of purpose and passion to be in his posse. In other words, men can't help you find your purpose if they aren't living theirs. The men you choose don't have to be close friends, but they must be superior men.

Authors of Aspiration. The third way you can clarify the direction of your life is to read books written by those who are experts at helping others find their deepest purpose. I recommend the following: *The Way of the Superior Man,* by David Deida; *True Purpose*, by Tim Kelley; *5 Wishes*, by Dr. Gay Hendricks; *The Power of Full Engagement*, by Jim Loehr.

Do whatever it takes to discover why you're alive. Mark Twain put it this way: *"The two most important days in your life are the day you were born and the day you find out why."* Use one or more of these three methods to find out why.

(2) Lead Your Relationship—Strength of Presence

I often joke that I'm like Mel Gibson's character in the movie, *What Women Want.*[80] It's about a guy who has an accident and is able to hear women's innermost thoughts. Now, I can't actually read women's minds, but because they talk to me about men and their love lives all day, every day, I've got a pretty good idea what they're thinking. And if I had to summarize their #1 complaint about men it would be this:

---

[80] Here's the movie's trailer, in case you aren't familiar with it: http://bit.ly/1nwJnLj

They feel confused as to how a man feels about them and what his intentions are for their relationship.

One of the hallmarks of a single superior man is that a woman always knows exactly how he feels about her and what kind of relationship he wants, moment-to-moment, stage-to-stage. She has absolutely no doubt as to where he stands. So, for example, if a woman has to initiate "the talk"— if she has to ask how you feel about her, or if she has to ask if you want to date her exclusively, or if she has to ask if you want to take your profiles down—if a woman has to ask any of that, you have failed at being a superior man. She wants to feel the strength of your presence, which means she wants you to lead the relationship. *She should never have to ask you to define the relationship, no matter what stage it's in.*

Relationships follow a progression. They move through stages. The first stage might be called the approach stage. Someone has to make the first move, whether it's online or in person. The second major stage is whether or not there will be a second date. Once you start seeing each other regularly, the third stage might be exclusivity. The fourth stage is when the relationship becomes sexual,[81] and the fifth stage might be when you meet each other's friends and family. And the final stage is when some kind of formal commitment is made either by moving in together or proposing marriage.

Just as it's the Masculine's role to propose marriage, it's the Masculine's role to "propose" at every stage of the relationship.

The Masculine partner in a relationship is responsible for the growth and movement of a relationship through its various stages. A superior man "proposes" a date; he "proposes" exclusivity; he "proposes" that the relationship becomes sexual, and so on. In other words, it's the Masculine's role to say, "This is how I feel and this is where I want to take you. Do you want to go there with me?" A superior man never waffles and wavers, leaving the woman to wonder what's happening.

However, leading your relationship and taking charge of its development does not mean you have to move from stage to stage. You have to

---

[81] Your sexual boundaries are none of my business, but if you're looking to attract a long-term relationship, I suggest that people wait to become sexual at least until the relationship becomes exclusive. To do so earlier often results in a lot of pain.

want that, of course. And that's the point. Tell her what you want—moment to moment. If you don't think the relationship is viable, tell her why and end it. If you're not ready to take the next step, tell her so and explain why. And if you are ready to take things to the next level, look her in the eye and invite her into that new space.

(3) Love Your Woman—Openness of Heart

One of the points I've made in this section of the book is that if a woman can learn how to support a man's mission through her radiant life force, she won't be single for long. The same goes for us men. If we learn how to support a woman's desire for love, through the openness of our hearts, then we won't be single for long either. So I want to share some very practical ways to love a woman and fulfill her desire for love.

Hands. I use the word "hands" to refer to your entire physical openness with a woman. Remember, she's a sensual creature. She lives in her body and through her senses. So if you want to connect with a woman, you must know how to use your body. Yes, that means sexually, but only if your relationship is at that stage or beyond. If your relationship is at an earlier stage, she will feel the openness of your heart through your posture, eye contact, non-sexual touching and breath.

When you're talking with a woman, in any setting, make sure you're facing her directly with your spine erect. Gaze into her left eye (it's the eye of receptivity), synchronize your breath with hers and touch her in a way that's appropriate to what she's expressing and the stage your relationship is in. Obviously, the earlier the stage, the less touching there is. These physical things will allow her to feel your open heart. A total turn on for her.

Hearing. Do not fix her or offer suggestions, even if she asks you to, at least not initially. The first thing you want to do is feel her and you do that by listening. Ask her questions like, "Say more about that," or "So what happened next?" Also, guess at her feelings by saying something like, "Wow, that must have really hurt," and if you're listening, you'll be right. When you can mirror her feelings back to her, she'll feel seen, which is about the sexiest feeling in the world to a woman.

Humor. A skill that a superior man uses *with great caution and consciousness* is his sense of humor. While it's always good to make a woman laugh, the superior man knows how to use humor to shift a woman's mood from closure to openness, from darkness to radiance. Your presence has to be very strong, however, because your humor could be taken as making light of her feelings. But there are times when humor can set her free and if

200

you're present enough to know when, how and if to use this tool, she'll see it as an expression of the openness of your heart.

Heart. The Masculine gift is to offer direction in the midst of chaos. This direction comes from a man's heart. There is a time for a man's "river banks" to guide a woman's flow, but this always comes after he first has used his "hands," "hearing," and "humor." The first three "H's" reveal your open, present heart and they earn you the right to offer direction. This skill is mostly used in the latter stages of a relationship. Rarely will you ever direct a woman's emotional flow on a first date. That's a sure fire way to make it your last date. You simply have not earned the right to penetrate her life to that degree. In other words, she doesn't trust you that deeply yet, nor should she.

Conclusion

So, there it is guys. A few practical ways to increase and express the depth of your clarity, presence and openness in your relationships with women. It won't do you any good to merely know them; you must do them and you must do them consistently. But if you do, you will be irresistible to radiant woman because you'll be a superior man.

Attraction Factors

1. Which purpose-finding strategy are you going to use to clarify your mission? When will you do it?

2. Do a mental audit of your current relationships. Does each woman know exactly how you feel and the intention you have for the two of you? If not, when will you clarify that for her?

BARRIER SEVEN

CREATION
The Art of Effortless Manifestation

"Your imagination is your preview of life's coming attractions."

~ Albert Einstein

This final section of the book is called The Art of Effortless Manifestation, with the emphasis on *effortless*, because once you've removed the first six barriers, love can and will flow into your life without you having to do much. As Rumi said, *"Your task is not to seek love,* but merely to seek and find all the barriers within yourself that you've built against it." Now that you've done that, I would expect you to meet someone very soon, if you haven't already.

So the final barrier is not being clear about what you want and how you plan to manifest it. Even though the conscious dater doesn't play games, he or she does have a plan, a conscious M.O., if you will, that even extends to online dating.

Here's how this final section breaks down:

Chapter 29: Begin with the End in Mind
Chapter 30: New Beginnings
Chapter 31: A Crash Course on Internet Dating

Begin With The End In Mind

"To begin with the end in mind means to start with a clear understanding of your destination...It's based on the principle that all things are created twice. There's the mental or first creation, and a physical or second creation to all things...You have to make sure that the blueprint, the first creation, is really what you want, that you've thought everything through."

~ Stephen R. Covey

Attracting lasting love is like running a marathon. If you want to finish, your focus should be on training for the race, not running it. Focusing on race day strategies like warming up, pacing, drafting and hydration is pointless if you haven't properly prepared. You have to be physically fit; that's the most important thing, by far. However, if you have trained properly, if you are fit, then thinking about racing strategy is important.

That's where we are in this book. You're in shape, your training is complete, and because of that, it's finally appropriate to talk about "race day strategies."

Beginning with the end in mind means, (1) Creating your list, (2) Writing your relationship vision and (3) Setting your sexual boundaries. Let's talk briefly about each one.

(1) Creating Your List

Once you've worked on yourself, it's important to create a list of qualities you want in a life partner. But before we get into creating your list, it's essential that you know what its purpose is. It's not to define who you'll be in a long-term committed relationship with—your relationship vision defines that—your list merely defines whom you will date.

Your list sets the boundaries as to who you will date,
not who you will commit to or marry.

In other words, your list will determine who is qualified or disqualified from even dating you. This list, what I call "Absolute Yeses and Noes," defines the playing field of your love life. They are the foul lines or the sidelines, if you will. A person must be within these lines for you even to date them. In other words, if a person doesn't impeccably fulfill every single one of your Yeses and Noes, you won't even date them, much less marry them.

Your list of Yeses and Noes must be very short (no more than 3-5 of each), and every one of them must be critically important to you and non-negotiable. In other words, they are the type of things over which women would dump, say, Adam Levine or George Clooney, and men would dump Jennifer Anniston or Jennifer Lopez.

Now, you might be thinking, *what kinds of things could be THAT important?* Well, issues pertaining to religion, children, smoking or having a job, might be a few. In other words, they're very important things.

I searched my computer and found my list of absolute Yeses and Noes. It was written in 2006, the year I met my wife. Here's exactly what I wrote, and they are in order of importance.

Yeses...
1. She's devoted to her personal growth
2. She's fun to be around and I enjoy her personality
3. She's emotionally and sexually available
4. She reveals rather than conceals

Noes...
1. She's not a smoker or an addict
2. She's not a blamer
3. She does not have children under 10
4. She's not financially dependent on me

I can honestly tell you that if Jennifer Anniston or Jennifer Lopez wanted to be in a relationship with me, I would refuse if they didn't fulfill every item on that list. They are THAT important to me. Non-negotiable. What are the things that are that important to you? (And make sure you live up to your own list! Don't ask for something that's not already true in your life.) Make your list now.

(2) Write Your Relationship Vision

Imagine that you're talking with a friend who you haven't seen in years, and since then you've met this incredible person and you are in the relationship of your dreams. You've been together and exclusive for about a year and it's everything you've ever wanted. Your friend, of course, is ecstatic for you and eager to hear all about it. So you describe everything about this amazing relationship you're in. Can you imagine that scenario? I want you to write down what you'd say.

The second major issue to focus on once you've released all your barriers is to write your relationship vision. This is a deeply emotional, heart-felt and fairly lengthy description (perhaps 500 words, or longer) of what you most want to experience with your ideal partner. It must be written or typed out. It cannot merely be imagined. Furthermore, not only do I want you to go into great detail, I want you to write from the present tense as if you're already in this amazing relationship.

What topics should be addressed? Well, here are 7 areas to touch on in your relationship vision:

Character. I want you to describe your partner in detail, going well beyond your Yeses and Noes. In other words, what is it about this person's character that makes you love them so much?

Chemistry. Describe the sexual attraction between the two of you. Why is he or she such a turn on to you? What is it about them that drives you wild?

Communication. This is a hallmark of a great relationship. Describe the openness and honesty between you, how you listen to each other and how you express your emotions.

Compatibility. Why are the two of you such a good fit? Perhaps you share similar values and goals. Perhaps you both want a certain kind of lifestyle. If there's something you've always wanted to share with a partner (e.g., tennis, traveling, antiquing, etc.), this is where you'd describe it.

Conflict. Every relationship experiences conflict. Good relationships know how to work through problems and form a deeper bond because of it. Describe how you fight, as well as how you handle stress and challenges.

Commerce. Describe your financial situation, including how much money you both make and how you handle money matters. Do you have separate or joint bank accounts? Is there a limit as to how much either partner can spend without discussing it with the other? Money is one of the major sources of conflict for couples. Describe how the two of you deal with it.

Consummation. What's your physical relationship like? How often do you have sex and how do you treat each other sexually, both in the bedroom and out? Do you flirt and have foreplay throughout the day, and if so, what does that look like? How are you romantic with your partner and how are they with you? Be specific. There's no need to discuss sexual technique (unless you want to), but definitely describe the feeling tone of your love life.

One word of warning: Because what you're writing about is not currently happening in your life, it will hurt like hell to write about it. Frankly, if you're not an emotional wreck when writing this, you're not really tuning into what you want. However, I'm not some sort of sadist. I don't want you to suffer, but writing your relationship vision is a necessary step in the manifestation process, and unfortunately, it's a painful one.

(3) Set Your Sexual Boundaries

There has been a sexual revolution going on in our culture for quite some time. It began with the "free sex" movement in the 1960's, which led to the "safe sex" movement of the 1980's, and now it's time for another shift, to something I call, "smart sex."[82]

I cannot tell you how many people I've worked with who have been devastated and heartbroken by their sexual choices. Since sex is such a huge part of the human experience, and since it is a source of so much pain, you must think this issue through. My role, of course, is not to tell you what your boundaries should be, but only to point you toward making smart sexual choices for yourself.

Sex is either a celebration of chemistry or a celebration of commitment.

This is a critical insight and one that you really need to understand and come to terms with. When two people meet and experience intense chemistry, they can decide to celebrate those feelings by having sex together. When that happens, it doesn't mean a relationship is starting or that the two people will even want to see each other again. It just means they're physically attracted to each other. It does NOT mean they want more than that necessarily. They are simply attracted to each other and they're celebrating that.

However, sex can also celebrate that some kind of commitment has been made, that a relationship has developed and progressed to a certain stage. Some of those stages might be things like taking your profiles down, or becoming an exclusive couple, or dating for a certain amount of time, or moving in together, or getting engaged, or even getting married. When a

---

[82] Here's a link to a blog piece I wrote on conscious sex: http://bit.ly/1vzyud7

relationship has reached any of those stages, that's when you may decide to engage sexually. In other words, you're celebrating a commitment, not chemistry.

Whichever you do is fine. The point is that you must know what your sexual activity means; you need to be smart when it comes to sex. Set your boundaries and stick to them. Are you going to celebrate chemistry or commitment? While I have no moral issue with either choice, in my experience, when people wait until there's some form of commitment made, I hear far fewer horror stories.

Attraction Factors

1. Write your absolute Yeses and Noes.

2. Write your relationship vision on a separate piece of paper or in a Word doc.

3. What are your sexual boundaries? Answer it this way: I will have sex when (blank) happens.

30

New Beginnings

"Do you want to meet the love of your life? Look in the mirror."

~ Byron Katie

Let's get down to the nitty-gritty. Having released all our barriers, decided who we want, visualized our relationship as if it already exists and set our sexual boundaries, we're finally ready to "get out there." But that raises a lot of questions, too. Where do we go to meet the person who fulfills our Yeses and Noes and stars in our relationship vision? And, if I am able to find them, how do I approach them, and more importantly, what do I say? This chapter will answer all three of those questions.

(1) Where To Go

Where do you go to meet your ideal partner? Well, if you've been reading this book, especially the section on Masculine/Feminine dynamics, then you should already know what I'm going to say.

Principle #1: It doesn't matter where you go; it only matters HOW you go.

When it comes to attraction, your energy is far more important than your location. Where you hang out is irrelevant. It's the condition of your life and the openness of your heart that matters. Listen to David Deida (men, this applies to you too, simply flip the words around):

> "You always attract and inspire a man as deeply committed to opening in love as you are—right now—which means that a man will be as actively present with you as you are actively radiating your love and allowing your yearning heart to open in his company."

It doesn't matter where you go. If you're not radiant, you'll attract mediocre men. If you're not superior, you'll attract closed women. Wondering where to go is the wrong question. Wonder, instead, about how radiant or superior you are. Attraction is not like real estate. It's not "location, location, location." It's "energy, energy, energy."

Principle #2: Focus on authenticity not strategy.

I have been working in the field of attraction, dating and intimacy for a long time and I've learned that relationship advice for single people usually falls in one of two categories. Relationship experts are either telling you how to play the game better or they challenge the game altogether.

I am squarely in the (microscopic) camp of those who challenge the game altogether. I'll talk more about this later when I get to "What To Say," but know that the only "strategy" or "technique" used by a radiant woman or a superior man is authenticity.

I often joke with my clients that no matter what the relationship question is, the answer is always the same—be authentic. "This is what happened, what do I do?" Be authentic. "He said this to me, what should I say?" Be authentic. "How do I handle this situation?" Be authentic. "I'm feeling frustrated (or scared or confused or hurt or disappointed), what should I do?" Be authentic. Authenticity is the "game" of the conscious dater.

Principle #3: Prioritize the personal over the digital.

Even though it's said that 70% of single people are online, I want to encourage you to prioritize the personal ways of meeting people over the digital ways. I'm not totally against online dating; I just don't want you to put all your eggs in that basket. Here's why.

Chemistry and compatibility are the two major parts of any intimate relationship and you need both to make a relationship work. However, in my experience, the order in which they occur is important. When you meet someone in the normal course of life, chemistry happens first and compatibility happens second. But when you meet online the order is reversed. People can spend weeks getting to know each other via profiles, pictures, emails, text messages and phone calls and then when they finally meet, they discover there's no chemistry.[83] A lot of time and energy has been wasted.

So, although there are online success stories, and I'll show you how to have one of your own in the next chapter, I still recommend the personal ways of meeting people over the digital ways.

---

[83] Chemistry cannot be determined via pictures. It's an energetic phenomenon that can only happen face-to-face.

Here are some places to go that prioritize the personal over the digital: Speed Dating events,[84] Lock and Key Events,[85] social or business events, networking events, Meet Up groups, churches, coffee shops, bookstores, bars and clubs.

Principle #4: Look for love as you're living your life.

There was a time in my life when everything I did was based upon how likely I was to meet a woman. I didn't go to events because I wanted to go; I went because I thought SHE might be there. I chose restaurants, not because I wanted to eat there, but because SHE might be eating there. I chose bars all the way across town if I thought SHE might be there. I'd go listen to a band, not because I liked their music, but because I thought SHE did. On and on it went.

Everything was about finding a woman. But then, because of the work I did with my coach, all of which is chronicled in my first book, *I made the shift from looking for love to living my life.*

The first major thing I did after having made that shift was to go to that personal growth conference I mentioned in the Prologue. I didn't go there because SHE might be there (even though she was). I went because I wanted to hear the speaker, Dr. Kathlyn Hendricks. I would never have gone there if my priority was to find a woman because the Hendricks' work is focused mainly on couples. I went because *I* wanted to go.

But, and this is hugely important, I was certainly open to meeting someone *and I was energetically ready to do so.* I walked in that room clear, present and open.

I was living my life and I was living it in a superior way and the universe did the rest. The goal of this book is to get you to do the same.

So, what do you love to do? What are your interests and hobbies? What makes you happy and alive? Do that. Do things that open your heart. Go to *Meet Up* groups that are focused on something you're truly interested in, not those that might have a bunch of single men or women in attendance. Choose a church that is aligned with your faith, but if there's more than one of those, then choose the one with a bigger single's group. Go to singles events or workshops, get involved in organizations, charities or causes, take yoga or spin classes, join a cycling or running group, learn to Tango or Sal-

---

[84] http://www.pre-dating.com
[85] http://www.lockandkeyevents.com

sa, play golf or tennis—*but do it because you want to do it, not because you want to meet someone.*

Look for love as you live your life. Don't get it backwards. Don't live your life looking for love. Your job is to be radiant or superior. It's the universe's job to bring your ideal partner to you when the time is right.

(2) How To Approach

When you do find yourself in a "target rich environment," as *Maverick* (Tom Cruise) put it in *Top Gun*, here are 4 principles to consider when approaching someone.

Principle #1: The Masculine Approaches but the Feminine Chooses.

One of the most memorable things my coach, Diana, ever said to me was an off-handed comment about dating. She said, "Women always choose the man. It's just that the smart women make the man think it was his idea."

She was saying that although it's traditional for a man to initiate and physically approach a woman, she's far from passive in the process. In fact, she's choosing him first, non-verbally.

The Feminine is a genius at non-verbal communication and she can influence a man's behavior through subtle and almost subliminal things like smiling, lingering eye contact or a slight gesture like twirling her hair or a tilt of her head. She's saying, "come talk to me" without saying it. Men don't always consciously pick up on such subtle invitations (they're not nearly as attuned to the energetic level as women are), they just start to feel confident about approaching her, not knowing that she's already chosen them.

Years later, when they're married and someone asks them how they met, he'll say he bravely walked up to her and started a conversation and she'll smile, knowing full well that she chose him.

Now, this is not to say a woman cannot or should not walk up to a man and say, "You're really handsome and I'd like to buy you dinner Saturday night and get to know you better." A woman can do that. There are no rules. However, by doing that, she's in her Masculine (initiating and presenting a plan is Masculine no matter what gender does it), which will force him into his Feminine, and if he has a Feminine essence and she has a Masculine essence, they will be extremely attracted to each other. But if that's not true, she'll either get shot down, or worse, a slow depolarization will begin and the relationship will probably fizzle out in a few weeks and wind up in the Friend Zone.

So, the Masculine does the approaching, but the Feminine does the choosing in her wonderfully seductive and subtle ways.

Principle #2: Dress for success.

I'm around single people quite a bit, both privately in coaching sessions, but also publically at events, and I'm amazed at how both men and women sabotage themselves when it comes to their attire.

Take men, for instance. You'll remember from the last section, that one of the things women find sexy in a man is his ability to pay attention and be present. When a man is not appropriately dressed for either the occasion or the location, he's telling a woman that he's not paying attention. So women are turned off physically because the guy doesn't look good, but more importantly, they're turned off energetically.

Women are better in this area, but they too can sabotage themselves. It's not uncommon for women to complain that men see them as sex objects. Part of that is on men, of course, but if a woman is dressed in a CFM outfit (come fuck me), she's "advertising" her sexuality and men will buy what she seems to be selling. While the Feminine is about radiance and a woman wants to be beautiful and attractive, a radiant woman pays very close attention to how provocatively she dresses. There's no right and wrong here. I'm simply encouraging you be conscious of the message you're sending and don't be surprised when it's received.

Principle #3: Look at yourself!

Some men don't ever seem to look in a mirror because if they did, they'd notice things like their teeth need to be better taken care of or that they have hair growing out of places it shouldn't. Being groomed, taking a shower and having fresh breath—unfortunately, men need to be reminded of these things.

Women don't need to be told to notice their physical appearance. That comes quite naturally. They do, however, need to notice their energetic appearance. If they could see their affect and attitude in a mirror, they'd notice their body language, facial expressions and the way they speak is turning men off, or worse, telling them to stay away. Radiant women smile, play and flirt. Yet far too often, women don't notice that they appear unapproachable.

So both genders need to look in the mirror—men to notice their physical appearance and women to notice their energetic appearance.

Principle #4: Work on your blocks.

This entire book has been about barriers and blocks, so I won't belabor the point any further, except to say that you must do whatever it takes to release things like shyness, lack of confidence, the fear of rejection, trust issues and so on. You won't approach others if those issues remain in your life and others won't approach you. You have to end your self-sabotaging patterns. That's the whole point of this book.

(3) What To Say

I did a quick Google search looking for cheesy pick up lines and I found dozens. Here are a few that I found funny, in a creepy sort of way:

- "Is it hot in here or is it just you?"
- "I've got skittles in my mouth, wanna taste the rainbow?"
- "Do you believe in love at first sight, or should I walk by again?"
- "Can I have your picture so I can show Santa what I want for Christmas?"
- "Even if there wasn't any gravity on earth, I would still fall for you!"

Now, those are kind of funny, but as you might assume, using cheesy lines does not fall in the realm of conscious communication. Superior men don't use them and radiant women don't respond to them. However, there is a place for humor, flirting and playfulness. In certain situations, using one of those lines to be *intentionally* cheesy can be quite charming. Let's not take ourselves too seriously and take all the fun out of relationships, dating and flirting. Playfulness and humor are very attractive qualities.

Now that we know where to go and how to approach, let's finish this chapter by talking about what to say. Here are three principles that can help you know what to say at the very beginning of a relationship.

Principle #1: Recognize the importance of the first 10 seconds.

The most powerful moment in any relationship is what happens in the first 10 seconds because it sets the tone and determines the way the entire relationship is going to go. That is not an overstatement. It's important that you don't underestimate the creative power of the first 10 seconds. You're determining the type of relationship you're going to have by what you say or don't say.

So, let me ask you this: What kind of relationship do you want? What's your relationship vision? If you want a relationship that will ultimately be about games, confusion, dishonesty, deception or manipulation, then start it that way by using a pick up line, or play some sort of game right from the start. You'll end up with a game-playing relationship. Or start off saying something dishonest—about yourself or them or the way you feel or your relationship status or your job. You'll end up with a dishonest, manipulative relationship.

But if you want an honest, open, authentic relationship where the two of you come from your hearts, then the first words out of your mouth need to be honest, authentic and from the heart.

What you say in the first 10 seconds has to be congruent with your relationship vision. In other words, begin with the end in mind.

My last two significant relationships illustrate this beautifully. When I met my fiancée, I was still married and I lied to her about that. Although that came out within a few weeks, we stayed together for 30 months and became engaged. But our relationship was doomed by my initial deception. It never really had a chance. We were never able to create an honest, authentic intimacy because it wasn't started that way. A relationship is like a train. Once it gets going in a certain direction, it's really hard to stop it and it's nearly impossible to turn it around.

Fast forward to the conference I wrote about in the Prologue. From the moment MaryMargaret and I met, we were open, honest and vulnerable with each other, doing creative joint play and sharing our personas with each other. That's about as authentic as it gets and our relationship has been like that ever since.

Now, do not misunderstand what I'm saying. You probably will not meet in the way we did and you won't talk about your personas like we did either, at least not right away. Frankly, if we had met in any other context we wouldn't have talked about that stuff so soon either. But even if we had met in a bar, our conversation would have been open, honest and vulnerable, which leads to the second principle.

Principle: #2: Speak authentically.

Say something that is real, authentic and from your heart in the first 10 seconds. Whatever is going on inside of you, whatever thoughts you're having, whatever feeling you're experiencing, *say that*. Live out loud. Make your inner conversation public, tune into your body and your experience and come forward with that. *Just be real.*

For example, if you like the way a person is dressed, or if you like their hairstyle or their smile, tell them. Compliments are always good, if they're genuine.

If you've had to work up the courage to talk to someone and you feel a knot in your stomach because you're so nervous, tell them that. "Hi, I have spent the last 15 minutes working up the courage to come over here and I've got a knot in my stomach I'm so nervous. I'm Roy. What's your name?" If you want to meet someone but you have absolutely no idea what to say, walk up to them and say, "Hi, I've been wanting to meet you and I have absolutely no idea what to say. I'm Roy. What's your name?"

If you see someone you're really attracted to, but it's in a random place like a mall, a grocery store or the post office and you don't have time to talk, go up to them and say, "Excuse me. I know this is sort of an awkward situation and neither one of us probably has time to talk right now, but wow, I think you're beautiful (or handsome) and I'd love to have a cup of coffee with you sometime. Would you be interested in that?"

If you'd like some guy to buy you a drink, go up to him and say, "If you asked to buy me a drink, I think I'd say yes," and playfully wink at him. If someone finally asks for your number and inside you go, "YES!" live out loud. Say, "Hell yes. I'd love to get together with you. I was hoping you'd ask."

The examples are endless, but in every situation the "strategy" is simply to tell them exactly what's going on inside of you. Be honest, authentic and come from your heart.

Some people love this approach, realizing how effortless and simple it is, but most are scared to death by it. They don't want to expose their true feelings. They don't want a person to know that they lack confidence or that they fear rejection. They don't want to let on how totally excited they are about someone for fear that they could be taken advantage of or seem desperate.

I understand those feelings but to do anything else is to play games. There are only two choices in the dating scene: You're either playing games (to one degree or another) or you're being authentic. The choice is yours. But make no mistake: The way you start a relationship will determine the kind of relationship it will become.

Principle #3: Let the Golden Rule guide you.

Superior men and radiant women end relationships, whether they're 3 minutes long or 3 years long, respectfully and honestly, following the Golden Rule—"do unto others as you would have them do unto you."

No one likes those awkward, and perhaps, emotional moments when you have to say "no" or end a relationship. Most of us will do almost anything to avoid that. But I'm sure you'd prefer to be told the truth rather than be given the "Houdini" treatment. So treat others the way you want to be treated. Don't disappear on people and don't deceive them either. Be honest and authentic, even when you're ending a relationship.

Attraction Factors
1. There were 4 principles given in the section addressing "Where To Go." Which one resonated with you the most and what are you going to do about it?

2. There were 4 principles given in the section addressing "How To Approach." Which one resonated with you the most and what are you going to do about it?

3. There were 3 principles given in the section addressing "What To Say." Which one resonated with you the most and what are you going to do about it?

— 31 —

A Crash Course on Internet Dating

"I don't have Ex's, I have Y's. Like, Y the hell did I date you?"

~ Kevin Hart

Millions of single people are involved in Internet dating and so this book wouldn't be complete if it didn't touch on how to attract lasting love—online. My goal is to give you a crash course on how to avoid horror stories and create a love story online.

I did online dating for about 18 months. I was on four different sites: *Match, E-harmony, Great Expectations* and *Yahoo Personals* (which I don't think exists anymore). I've also coached hundreds of people who've been online and I've learned a lot from their triumphs and tragedies as well as my own. So the wisdom I'm going to share has been gleaned from direct experience and I'm sure it will help you craft an online presence that will enable you to attract your ideal partner

This crash course has four parts: Principles, Practices, Profiles and Pictures.[86]

Principles

(1) Have a sense of humor.

You will have a lot of bizarre experiences online. Some will be hilarious; some will be horrendous. It goes with the territory. This crash course will help you reduce the horror stories, but it won't eliminate them. It's just not possible. You won't have to kiss a bunch of frogs, but you will definitely meet some. So you have to have a sense of humor about the whole thing.

(2) Be pickier than usual.

There are so many people online that if you contact or respond to everyone who seems "okay," you'll be overwhelmed. Between your career and the full life that you lead, you don't have time for "okay," so raise the bar and be pickier than usual. If you read a person's profile and it doesn't com-

---

[86] For a more thorough discussion, see my eCourse: *Finding Love Online.*

pletely resonate with you, don't meet them. Protect your time and your energy and only meet people who almost seem too good to pass up.

(3) Be absolutely honest.

Every single thing in your profile should be the truth, including (but not limited to) your age, your job status, and especially your relationship status. If you misrepresent yourself, even by a little, you're not only setting a deceptive and manipulative tone, which I just talked about, you're also revealing a complete lack of self-esteem on your part. When you lie about something, what you're saying is, "I don't think you'll like the person I am so I'm going to misrepresent myself and craft an image that I hope you will like." That's dark energy and it will attract someone who is also dishonest and lacking self-esteem.

(4) Give serious thought to your dating range.

It baffles me when people set their online distance range to more than an hour's drive or if they're willing to communicate with people in different states. Tell me, how does that work? If you want a long-term committed relationship, how do you ever see each other with enough frequency to seriously consider quitting your job and moving to be with them? Don't you have to date and see someone multiple times a week for at least 6 months to develop that kind of trust? (Answer: Yes!) How does that work if you don't live near each other?

There's no right or wrong here, but you should give this serious thought. Are you willing to move if the situation is right? The answer to that must be in your profile. And when you communicate with someone outside of your immediate area, your first conversation should be to determine who is willing to move, should things go well. If neither of you is willing to move, you must say goodbye immediately.

(5) Keep your residence and income private.

I'm a big proponent of honesty but not when it comes to where you live and how much money you make. There are appropriate times to reveal those things. Where you live and work might be revealed after 5 or more dates, while how much money you make might be revealed after 6 months of exclusivity. (I'm just making those time frames up arbitrarily to make a point.) You can and should tell a person how you authentically feel about them, but you don't share personal information until you've built a high degree of trust.

Practices

There are four critical practices that will keep you sane and reduce your chances of attracting horror stories into your life.

(1) Cut to the chase.

Don't get stuck in what I call "digital hell" emailing, texting and talking on the phone for weeks on end. Get to a face-to-face meeting as soon as possible, even if someone's out of state. Don't waste your time. Find out if you have any chemistry right away. Meeting quickly also eliminates the "catfish" syndrome, where you allow yourself to get played by some phony person.

I recommend this scenario: After initial contact is made (I like the guy to initiate, but a woman can send the first note too), the other person looks at their profile to check them out and sends an email response either way. (If you're not interested, tell them. Don't ignore them.) If you like them, you can email back and forth once or twice, but then phone numbers should be exchanged. When you talk, chat and get to know each other, of course, but by the time the first call ends, a date to meet should be set. There should be no more than one week from first contact to first meeting. Cut to the chase.

(2) It's a meeting not a date!

The first time you get together should be for 30 minutes at Starbucks or something like that. It's not a date. *It's a meeting.* There are no dinner and drinks. No matter how amazing they seem, don't commit to a dinner date or anything longer than 30 minutes. Why get locked into a long, expensive dinner when you may know within minutes that there's no chemistry? That's nuts. Arrange for a short meeting to determine chemistry and to verify that they are the person they've presented themselves to be.

Now, if you want to leave your schedule open after the short meeting so that you can turn your meeting into a date if it goes well, fine, but you don't tell the other person that upfront. If things go well, then you can tell them you're up for more if they are. But start with a short coffee-type meeting. It will save you a lot of cash and headaches. Trust me. I speak from experience.

(3) No sex.

Under no circumstances should you have sex the first time you meet. Even if the 30 minute coffee meeting turns into a romantic 6 hour dinner date, even if the chemistry is so thick you can cut it with a knife, even if the person seems sincere, even if you have the thought they are "the one," no sex. You're asking for trouble if you celebrate chemistry. Remember: Smart sex.

(4) Listen, listen, listen

You don't want to be suspicious when you first meet someone, but you do want your ears wide open. Listen for confirmation of your Yeses and Noes. If they aren't met, it's over. Listen as they talk about their past relationships. If they're not complete, it's over. (What are the signs? Well, if they've been divorced for less than a year, be careful. If you're the first person they've dated since a break up, be careful. If they're separated, or if they get emotional talking about an ex, positively or negatively, get up and leave.) Finally, listen for any inconsistency between what's in their profile or what they've said on the phone and what they're telling you in person. If you sense something is off, ask direct questions and if what you hear doesn't make sense, walk away.

Profiles

Writing a good profile begins by asking yourself a critical question: To whom are you writing? Most people make the mistake of writing to the masses of men or women on-line since that's who's going to read it. It's logical to think, "There are hundreds or even thousands of people who are going to read this, so I want to write something that is widely appealing and gives a general feel for who I am and what I'm looking for."

Read the very next sentence as if I was screaming it at you, because I am: *That is exactly what you DON'T want to do!!!*

> ***You don't want to appeal to the masses;***
> ***you want to appeal to just one person,***
> ***the person who appears in your relationship vision.***

When you sit down to write your profile, I want you to imagine that the person who stars in your relationship vision is sitting across the table from you and you're writing that individual person a very personal, heartfelt note about what you most want to give and receive in a relationship.

Many people feel queasy about putting their relationship vision in their profile, but that is exactly what I want you to do. Express your deepest heart. Put it out there. (The only thing you'll hold back is your description of your sex life, but everything else can and should be in your profile.) That means you're profile is going to be rather long and very personal.

If you want to attract a person of depth, openness and spirituality—a superior man or a radiant woman—what kind of person do you think they're scrolling through profiles looking for? Answer: An equally radiant or superior person. Like attracts like. Since no one writes profiles like this, when a superior man or a radiant woman comes across yours, it will jump off the screen at them.

A radiant woman or a superior man has 5 major sections in their profile.

Section #1: Connect emotionally.

People will rarely read more than the first paragraph of a profile, so it has to pop. Your first paragraph should express your understanding of the felt needs and the emotional state of your ideal partner. What's their life like? How do they feel about being single and the dating scene in general? What do they want? What are they missing? You want to show that you "get them," that you understand them. Once you've done that, tell them how you solve that problem. Here are two examples.

> A man might write:
>
> "I can imagine that managing your career and maybe even being a single parent is challenging to say the least. I'm sure your heart yearns, as mine does, for an intimate relationship that provides mutual support and even inspiration to expand our creative potentials and build deeply into our children's lives. I long to be with a woman who would allow me to touch her life with my sense of humor and Masculine presence as she touches mine with her love, radiance and tenderness. To give and receive such gifts is very much what I want to share with a woman.

> A woman might write:
>
> "Sexy, to me, is a man on a mission, a man who wants to make his life count for himself, those he cares about and even the world. Yet I'm sure being filled with such passion and purpose is challenging and even exhausting at times. I long to be with a deeply trustable and conscious man, one who needs my Feminine touch and one whose loving presence frees me to support and inspire his life with my smile, sensuality and sassiness."

How many profiles have you read that begin like that?

Section #2: Tell them about yourself.

The very first line in the second section of your profile should come right out and state the kind of relationship you ultimately want, which is probably a long-term, monogamous relationship and possibly marriage. You want to "thin the herd" and chase away those who want one-night stands or simple casual dating. You want to date only those who want the same ultimate outcome that you do.

The second thing this section clarifies is who you are. This is where you tell them all about yourself, including what you do for a living, your kid's ages, your religion or spiritual beliefs (if that's an important part of your life), your personality, interests and hobbies. Tell them all about you and your life.

Section #3: Share your relationship vision.

This is the meat of your profile. I want you to edit the sexual content out of your relationship vision (that will only invite shallow, one dimensional types) and perhaps shorten it a bit, but I want you to tell the person reading your profile what you're looking for and what you want to experience with them. (This is basically a longer version of your opening paragraph.)

It's got to be written with feeling, heart and depth. You want to be open and vulnerable and you want to speak in very intimate, personal ways. Pour out your heart, in other words. Tell them what you crave, tell them what you fear you'll never find or experience, tell them what you dream about, tell them what you want to give in a relationship.

Section #4: Convey your boundaries.

In this section, you'll share your Yeses and Noes, but do so in a positive way. Again, you're "thinning the herd." This is also the section where you'll clarify your feelings about children (do you want them or not) and anything else you think they would want to know. If you've got something going on that might make them not want to date you, tell them here. If you're separated, say that. If you've got some sort of serious medical issue or health constraint, say that. Don't waste their time. Tell them things that might be deal-breakers for them. I know that's hard, but remember: Do unto others as...

Section #5: Describe your online M.O.

In this final section you want to tell them how you'd like the entire online dating process to unfold. Tell them you'd like to exchange emails, then talk by phone and then meet for a 30-minute coffee date. Wrap up by inviting them to contact you.

Pictures

You need at least 2 pictures: A clear one of your face and one that shows the general shape of your body. They deserve to know what you look like. I suggest that you get them professionally done. Do not take "selfies." If you have kids, a special hobby, a dog or a favorite team, it's great to have pictures of that as well. But you must have the head and body shots. Both pictures must have been taken within the last 6 months. Do not ever interact with anyone who doesn't have a picture posted. It's a huge "red flag."

Attraction Factors

1. List 5 changes that you're going to make to your profile as a result of what you've read.

2. When will you do them?

CONCLUSION

Let Go

"To seek, expect, or demand love is not love at all. It is egoic neediness. Love wants nothing because it lacks nothing. Love does not seek love. It places no conditions on life and others. It simply recognizes itself everywhere, in everyone."

~ Scott Kiloby

Let go.

Let go of seeking love and just live your life. It's not your responsibility to find your partner. That's the universe's job. Your job is only to make sure you've released each and every barrier discussed in this book. The rest is out of your hands.

My wife and I met serendipitously, in the flow of living our lives, *but we were ready for each other.* We were (1) prepared for something real, (2) we had let go of the victim mentality, (3) we had taken our "foot off the brake," (4) we were complete with former lovers, (5) we had released our relationship personas, (6) we were animating our Masculine or Feminine energy, and (7) we were committed to the "strategy" of authenticity.

That's all we could do; it's all we needed to do and it's all you need to do too.

It's not enough to know about the 7 barriers. You must do the work necessary to release them. Do not let this book collect dust on your shelf. Work with these barriers, wrestle with them if need be, and call me if you need support.

As I said at the end of the Introduction, I was not able to navigate these 7 Barriers on my own. My coach and guardian angel, Diana, walked with me every step of the way, and I would be honored to be "Clarence" for you.

Commit to your freedom. Get out of your own way. Let go and let love find you.

And invite me to the wedding.

ACKNOWLEDGEMENTS

There are quite a few people who helped with the creation of this book and I deeply appreciate all of them.

The first is my wife, MaryMargaret. Thank you, sweetheart, for your Feminine input and all the wonderful, and sometimes difficult, discussions we had as this book was being written.

I also want to thank Diane Vivian for her work on the cover. Bringing your Feminine creativity to this project was very much needed. And if you, the reader, saw this manuscript before Maclean Kirkwood, Julianna Ormond, Mary Jo Johnson, Ellen Brickman and Odette Sirbu got their hands on it, you'd know why I'm so grateful for them too.

Finally, to all my clients: We've learned so much together over the years and I appreciate all of you very much. Thank you for working and wrestling with these concepts and applying them to your lives.

APPENDIX I

The Dating Manifesto:
7 Commitments of Conscious Dating

The Law of Attraction means, "like attracts like." In this context that means we always attract someone operating from the same set of commitments that we are. Below are the 7 commitments of conscious daters.[87] Also listed (in italics and in red, if you're reading the e-version) are their counter-commitments. These describe how most single people date and they are the root cause of drama and disappointment.

1. RESPONSIBILITY

I commit to taking full responsibility for every aspect of my dating experience, including the kinds of people I attract, how I'm treated and the patterns I experience. I understand that nothing is happening "to me," it's happening "by me."

I commit to blaming the people I date, and/or the entire dating scene for the way I'm treated and my overall dating experience. I commit to playing the role of victim, villain or hero and taking more or less than 100% responsibility for what's occurring in my love life.

2. CURIOSITY

I commit to meeting every dating experience with curiosity, seeing each person and interaction as an opportunity to learn and grow in self-awareness.

I commit to being certain that my stories and perspectives are true. I commit to being right. I commit to being defensive, especially when I am sure that I'm right.

3. CANDOR

I commit to revealing rather than concealing, meeting each dating and relationship experience with openness, honesty, authenticity and complete candor.

I commit to playing games by misleading or deceiving the people I date, withholding my truth (including facts, feelings, and things I imagine)

---

[87] Based on the work of Jim Dethmer and Diana Chapman: www.conscious.is

and speaking in a way that allows me to avoid, control or manipulate an outcome.

4. ALLIES

I commit to seeing the people I date, including my former partners, and all my dating circumstances, as allies and teachers, perfectly suited to help me learn the most important things for my growth.

I commit to seeing the people and circumstances in my dating experience as mistakes, baggage, enemies and impediments to having the relationship I want.

5. SCARCITY

I commit to believing that there is enough of everything, that there is no shortage or scarcity of men, women, love, romance, money, energy, time, etc.

I commit to a scarcity mentality, believing that finding my ideal partner is like finding a needle in a haystack. I commit to the belief that I have to "settle," lower my standards and accept "red flags," while relying on pure luck or obsessive effort to find my partner.

6. SOURCE

I commit to being the source of my needs, including my desire for love, security, worthiness, happiness, specialness and connectedness.

I commit to believing that those I date (and eventually my partner) are responsible for alleviating my loneliness and making me feel safe, wanted, seen, loved, happy, etc. I commit to manipulating, controlling or punishing those who don't give those things to me.

7. STORY

I commit to seeing that the opposite of my story is as true, or truer, than my original story. I recognize that objectivity is an illusion, that I interpret the world around me through the lens of my personality and past conditioning which gives my stories meaning.

I commit to believing that my stories, and the meaning I give them, are true. I commit to insisting that others agree with my stories. I commit to interpreting events as "proof" that my stories are, indeed, true.

ABOUT THE AUTHOR

Roy Biancalana is an author, speaker and certified relationship coach. His mission is supporting single people in the art of attracting and creating conscious relationships.

While Roy coaches clients directly by phone, Skype or in person, he has also created numerous high-quality, video-based eCourses that address the most relevant issues facing single people today.

Roy serves as the relationship expert for *Fox35 TV* in Orlando, Fl. and has appeared on numerous radio shows including, but not limited to, *Positive Living Radio Show, ESPN radio, Comcast Sports, Chicago, The Daily Buzz* and *Golf Channel.*

Roy grew up in Chicago, Illinois, and took up the game of golf at age 12. He attended *Louisiana State University* on a golf scholarship and graduated with a degree in Marketing. After graduation, Roy turned professional, played on the PGA Tour for 2 years, won 75 tournaments nationwide and was a 4-time Illinois Player of the Year. He also completed in 6 major championships, the last of which was the 2004 PGA Championship.

After a divorce in 2003, followed by a devastating break-up with his fiancée in 2005, Roy spent two years working with a relationship coach to break free of the 7 barriers described in this book. That process transformed his life, allowing him to meet, date and marry the love of his life, Mary-Margaret. Roy then left his life as a professional golfer to show others how to transform their relationships and attract lasting love too.

Roy has a son in college and he lives with his wife, MaryMargaret, near Orlando, Florida.

He offers a complimentary 30-minute coaching session to anyone who is interested in working with him.

Roy Biancalana
www.coachingwithroy.com
roy@coachingwithroy.com
407-687-3387